FA4

WAY *of*

Jacket

WAY *of*
The Chakras

Caroline Shola Arewa

Thorsons

Thorsons
An Imprint of HarperCollins*Publishers*
77–85 Fulham Palace Road
Hammersmith, London W6 8JB

The Thorsons website address is: www.thorsons.com

Published by Thorsons 2001

1 3 5 7 9 10 8 6 4 2

© Caroline Shola Arewa 2001

Caroline Shola Arewa asserts the moral right
to be identified as the author of this work

A catalogue record for this book
is available from the British Library

ISBN 0 7225 4039 6

Printed and bound in Great Britain by
Martins The Printers Limited, Berwick upon Tweed

Contents

Dedicated to all people seeking Inner Vision

Acknowledgements

I give thanks and praise to the creator, the most high. I thank my Ancestors for continued protection and guidance. Love and thanks to my family, immediate and extended. Love and thanks to my friends for lasting support. Special thanks to those who have taught me and those I have taught, may the circle of Eternal Spirit never be broken.

Introduction

Chakras are becoming increasingly recognized as fundamental to holistic healthcare. At the beginning of this new millennium we are enjoying an increased acceptance of all things sacred. Spiritual techniques, complementary medicine, the healing arts and methods of empowerment have all grown in popularity. We are re-aligning ourselves energetically with the universe and its dynamic dance.

As we search for ways to develop ourselves personally and spiritually the sacredness of life becomes more apparent. Scientists tell us, as the ancients told us before, that we, like all life, are merely 'energy in motion'. So if we learn to understand energy, we will begin to understand the very essence of life itself.

Chakras are like power stations, they create and maintain energy. Chakras are at the very core of our existence. They are central to all we say and do. Understanding the chakras has wide-ranging benefits. Once you understand the principles of the chakras you will have tools to enhance your physical health and well being. Your spiritual awareness will grow and you will have the potential to live your life in the divine, fulfilling way it was intended.

Your chakras are the key to unfolding many of life's secrets. All who choose to read a book like this one have reached a very special place in life; a place where everything is taking on more meaning. You realize that life has a pattern, a sacred organization, a harmonic rhythm. You are seeking to live life in accordance with your higher intelligence and develop spiritual wisdom. You need look no further. The chakras hold many answers to life's questions. They are an organizing principle. They are the fuel that gives power to life.

Learning how to work with the chakras can balance and energize your body, mind and spirit. This new-found understanding can totally transform your life. You can find courage where you knew only fear. You can rest in the joy of Self-love. Confidence can replace low self-worth. Numerous personal talents and qualities can be enhanced through working with the chakras.

The chakras can also offer healing on a physical level. As energy is enabled to flow more freely through your body, many ailments can be released. Disease is often an accumulation of dammed-up energy. When we learn how energy moves through the chakras we can begin to allow it to flow freely through our bodies, creating greater health.

Spiritually the chakras are very significant. They form a ladder of spiritual ascension. This ladder reaches from the limitations of the earth plane and the physical realms to the freedom and liberation that awaits us in the astral realms and beyond. Through the chakras we are free to explore many levels of altered consciousness. We can raise our awareness to great heights as did the sages and wise people of old. We too can connect with the infinite pool of everlasting wisdom and knowledge. In the divine stillness of the chakras we can rest in absolute bliss.

We are living in unique times, we have available to us a wealth of spiritual teachings. In ancient times the knowledge I share with you in this book would have required initiation and years of training. Today it is imperative that we advance spiritually to save our under-nourished souls. We must also learn to live in unity, loving each other fully and nurturing the dying planet on which we live. For this reason many teachings are now being made available to all who hear the calling, and who are ready to make meaningful life changes.

You need only read and follow the simple exercises in order to feel and experience the vibrating energy fields that are your chakras. I have worked in the healing arts for over 20 years. I help people create *fulfilled lives*. It is my pleasure to share with you the way of the chakras.

How to use this book

Reading the first three chapters will give you an overview of the chakra system. Chapter 4 offers information to help you get started on your personal journey through the chakras. Chapters 5 to 11 focus on the chakras individually. In these chapters each chakra is illustrated. There is a detailed listing of characteristics for each of the seven main chakras, which you can use as a reference to develop your own understanding of the chakra system. I explore how each individual chakra relates to your body, mind and spirit, including common ailments. Rebalancing exercises are provided for all of the chakras. To attain the best results, allow about one month to work on each chakra. Every time you practise the exercises their effect and resonance will be different.

Try to practise the exercises as you read the book. This will give you a good sense of your energy system. If you work consciously and listen carefully your chakras will speak to you. Listen carefully without dismissing what comes up and without judging your Self negatively. Everything in life happens for a purpose and is part of your unique unfolding. You are a Divine being with infinite potential, each day you move closer to letting your radiant Inner Light shine fully.

ONE

WHAT ARE
Chakras?

WAY of

Gift of Divinity

Chakras are your **G**ift **O**f **D**ivinity, they are your inner **GOD**. The very essence of who you are. Chakras are responsible for creating and maintaining your very existence. They are energy centres – vibrating wheels of cosmic light that bring physical form into being. Without the chakras we would not be here. It is the chakras that keep your heart beating. It is the chakras that cause you to take life-giving breaths. The energy that radiates from your chakras sets your thoughts and feelings in motion. Your very desire for spiritual knowledge and wisdom is a sign of the gentle opening of these divine energy centres.

Seven Major Chakras

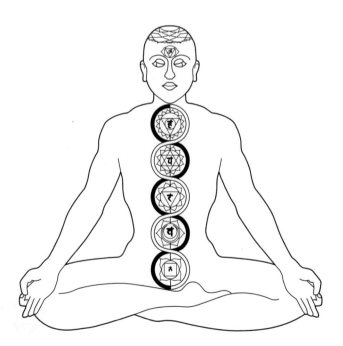

Chakra means wheel in Sanskrit and refers to cone-shaped vortices of energy, which spin and vibrate within the energy body. Humans are made up of many chakras. We have seven major, twenty-one minor, forty-nine minute and numerous minuscule chakras. They are wheels of divine light. The seven major chakras radiate out from different points along the spine, forming a vertical axis, which runs from the base of the spine to the top of the head. A pathway is produced that can transport us from the individual and personal realms of consciousness to the spiritual and universal realms.

We know the universe is made of energy. We know there is a Divine source of this energy that we call the creator. The creator has many names. God, Goddess, Oludamare, Ra, Grandfather Sky, Siva, are just a few of the names. Maybe you use another name. Despite the differing names the creator is only one. The creator is the source of all life; the primary source. From this primary source duality is created. And from this duality all life springs into being.

Prior to creation we were one with our creator. We reigned in absolute bliss. We knew no separation, no duality. We knew only Divine bliss. It is this bliss that we seek each and every day. We hold a memory of our divinity deep within our selves. This memory is imprinted in every cell. The problems we face in life arise because we choose to forget our Divine origins. We seek our pleasures in mundane activities and material wealth. We expect family, friends and lovers to arouse bliss in us. When people and property fail us, we suffer. From our ignorance we experience real pain. It is not until we awaken to our truth, the truth of our divine nature, that we can begin to live life fully. Ancient spiritual teachings inform us that when the creator decided to create

3

WAY of

life duality occurred. The pure undifferentiated energy of the creator split and became dual – the creator and the created, both of the same essence.

Yin and Yang

In Chinese spiritual tradition this duality is known as yin and yang. In Ancient Egypt it was called Nekhebet and Uatchet. In India it is called ida and pingala. These can all be translated respectively as negative and positive forces of energy. Chakras are magnetic fields that process these positive and negative forces of energy. Chakras have the ability to absorb energy from the universe and redistribute it throughout your system. This distribution of energy creates and then maintains our minds and our physical bodies.

Prana – The Life Force

Chakras are not only found in the human body, they are found in the body of the earth. They are found on the planets and throughout the universe. Chakras are present at all places where subtle energy is processed and stepped down into the creation of physical form. On earth there are many places of power. These are the chakras of our planet. They are places where energy is generated. In England, for example, there is a sacred town called Glastonbury. This is a spiritual power point in the country. Many feel this is the heart chakra of the country. Some go as far as to say it is the heart chakra of the earth. Mount Shasta in the US is thought to be the earth chakra of the planet and Giza in Egypt, home of the pyramids, is said to be the world's third eye.

Our bodies and the body of the earth are made up of a matrix of energy pathways. These pathways are called *nadis* in the body and *ley lines* on the earth. Nadis can be likened to arteries or veins in the physical body, which carry blood, only the nadis are subtle vessels and they carry prana or energy. These subtle vessels cannot be seen, and it is merely through their action that we know of their existence. Just as we know electricity exists when we plug the kettle into its supply, we cannot see the electricity; we know it exists because we witness its action.

Prana is the life-force. It is the subtle energy that flows through the nadis into the entire body and mind, keeping them animated and alive. Prana fuels the nervous system and the endocrine system. Together these two systems give rise to who we are. The nerves and hormones work in unison to orchestrate many of the body's functions. Energy then flows into the blood stream and gives rise to physical form.

5

Nadis

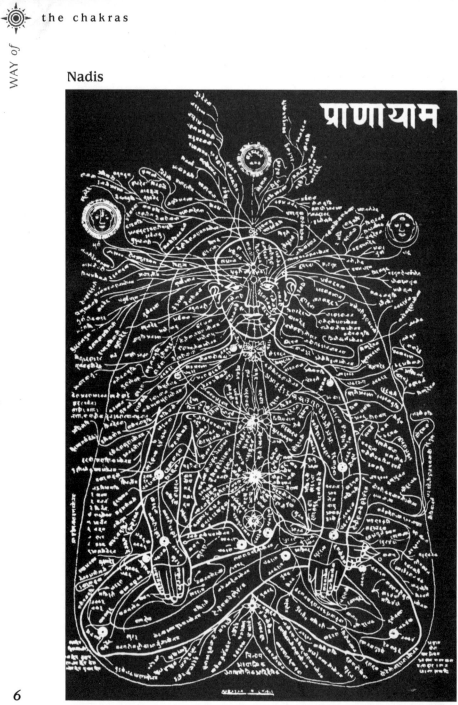

Step down flow of energy

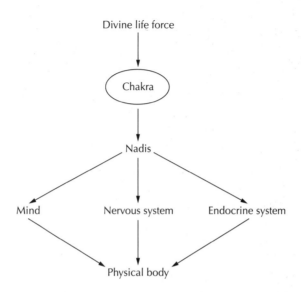

When we heal dis-ease holistically we always work to affect the flow of energy. When energy flows freely through the whole body it creates harmony and releases dis-ease. Chakras and energy underpin our physical form. Through balancing the chakras and improving the flow of energy we create change from the core, which is our energy system, to the periphery, which is the physical body.

Chakras are the central energetic core of our existence. It is this very core that links us to every living entity and connects us to our creator. The chakras unite us with our ancestors, spirit guides and helpers who bestow blessings upon us. The wisdom of past, present and future is revealed to us when we open the chakras more fully. Knowledge of the chakras can be used for personal development, healing, and transformation.

7

WAY of

The chakras hold the key to spiritual awakening, psychological well-being and physical health. Each of the seven chakras governs a different stage of psychological and spiritual development creating various levels of consciousness. The first three chakras – root, sacral and solar plexus – are responsible for survival, self-awareness and inner-stability respectively. The heart centre, which is fourth, is the point of transformation from the inner world, our personal reality, to the universal reality. The three remaining centres – throat, brow and crown – are spiritual centres focusing on communication, insight and wholeness. Physically, every chakra has various body parts under its control. The seven chakras govern the seven main sets of endocrine glands and in this way influence the entire harmony and equilibrium of the body.

The chakras resonate with the colours of the rainbow. The root chakra is red and the crown is violet, the other colours resonating with the chakras in between. Next time you see a full rainbow shining brightly in the sky, notice how it connects heaven and earth. Rainbows seem to reach down from the sky and touch the earth. This is like the chakras; they too provide a shining inner light that bridges the gap between heaven and earth. The crown chakra reaches heaven, while the root keeps us connected to our mother the earth. Chakras are our inner rainbow, they are GOD, the **G**ift **O**f **D**ivinity that resides within. When you open to this inner gift it will brighten up your life.

How the Chakras Affect your Spirit, Mind and Body

The chakras profoundly affect your spirit, mind and body. It is through the chakras that these aspects of your being are connected and can be aligned and balanced. The chakras are not in the physical body, they are part of the subtle energy body. They do, however, have direct correspondences in body and mind. This is a good time to introduce you to a simple exercise that will allow you to experience the chakras for yourself. Read through the following exercise and then take some time to enjoy it.

Hand Energy Sensing Exercise

Hand energy sensing exercise

WAY of

Take some time for yourself in a silent space. It can be out in the open or in a quiet room. Sit comfortably, either cross-legged on the floor or, if that is difficult, upright in a chair with both feet flat on the floor. Straighten your spine – this allows the chakras to sit one on top of the other in alignment. If you cannot straighten your back, do not worry, do the best you can. Support your back if necessary using cushions. Place your hands, palms facing upwards, on your knees. Close your eyes and take a few deep breaths. Begin to let your body relax. Remain upright and release any tightness. Feel the contact of your body with the floor and feel as though you are gently sinking into the ground more and more. Relax your shoulders and allow them to open. Feel your chest expand, lift your spine and take up more space in your body.

Now bring your attention to the point just below your navel; feel the sensation of energy or visualize a healing colour. Slowly begin to draw your energy or colour up from below the navel through the abdomen and chest. Feel the energy move and direct it around each of your shoulders and along your arms to your hands. Be still and feel the sensation of energy in your hands. When you feel a sensation in your hands, lift them up from your knees and turn them to face each other. Begin to bring your hands very slowly together, sensing the energy. Explore the space between your hands. The more subtly and imperceptibly you move your hands, the more powerfully you feel the energy. Draw your hands slowly together until they touch. Then very slowly return your hands to your knees. Take a few deep breaths and remain with your eyes closed for a moment.

Through this exercise you can feel the minor chakras of your hands and sense the energy field around your body, which is known as the aura. The sensation in your hands is from the minor chakras – it may be of heat, tingling, excitation – these centres are used in healing. As you draw your hands together you may encounter a resistance, a sense of something solid between your hands. This is the electromagnetic field – your aura, that permeates and embraces your body. If nothing is felt during the first few times you practise 'hand energy sensing', don't give up. It may just be that your concentration needs to be a little more focused on feeling within. Possibly you moved your hands too far, too fast. Continue practising the exercise and slowly you will develop your awareness of energy and the chakras.

Hopefully this experience has given you a felt sense of the chakras. Let us now continue looking at how the chakras affect us in spirit, mind and body. Each chakra has many characteristics associated with it. They pertain to spiritual, psychological and physical aspects of our being. Developing a felt sense of the chakras and understanding their characteristics can enhance your overall quality of life.

Spiritually, chakras are our core energy. As this core energy disperses out into your body it vibrates at different frequencies. The root chakra is the densest and the crown is the subtlest. These vibrations give rise to various elements, which are expressed through the chakras. Colours, as I mentioned earlier, are also determined by the different frequencies of energy. The chakras also resonate with deities and symbols. These spiritual characteristics represent specific qualities of energy that can be awakened at each of the different energy centres.

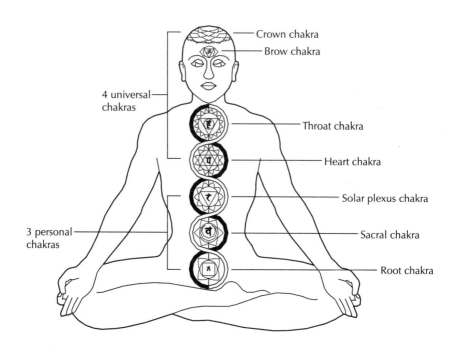

Crown chakra
Brow chakra
4 universal chakras
Throat chakra
Heart chakra
Solar plexus chakra
3 personal chakras
Sacral chakra
Root chakra

The first three chakras affect us in a personal way, while the remaining four are universal in their effect on us. The spiritual quality of the root chakra is grounding. This chakra is responsible for allowing you to incarnate fully into your physical vehicle. The energy which flows through it will affect your relationship to your body and the earth on which you stand.

The spiritual quality of the sacral chakra is centring. *'Being centred is the ability to move from or stay in a place of quiet inner wisdom.'*[1] It is about knowing, trusting and loving your inner Self.

The third chakra, at the solar plexus, is responsible for personal power, it is a feeling centre, a place where an abundance of energy is processed. When the four universal chakras (heart to crown) are not fully open personal power is often abused. When the solar plexus chakra is working in harmony with the other chakras it can be used in a positive way that can enrich you, the people around you and the planet we all share.

The universal chakras have more profound spiritual effects. The heart chakra marks a major transition point. It is situated between the three personal chakras, which lie below the heart, and the three universal chakras, which lie above it. The heart chakra, which sits in the middle of the seven wheels of light, is the centre of love and compassion.

The throat chakra is a centre of communication on many levels, for example, it connects us with the ancestral realms, angelic forces, nature and other divine beings. Opening the throat chakra more fully can help clarify our direction in life and provide us with the spiritual guidance we need.

The third eye is a powerful centre of insight and wisdom. It is the centre of inner vision. The crown chakra at the top of the head is the seat of perfect bliss. It is the place where we unite again with our creator and become one.

Psychologically the chakras take us on a journey through many emotions and experiences. E-motions are simply movements of energy. They are *energy in motion* that we interpret as happy, sad, angry, fearful, mad, etc. At each chakra different emotions are experienced. As we ascend our awareness through the chakras we move from limiting emotions such as fear and pain through to liberating emotions such as freedom and ecstasy. Journeying through the chakras helps us develop psychologically. We can move from a place of fear to one of courage, from anger to forgiveness. We can come to know ourselves more deeply and learn to love and respect who we really are. We can understand and build compassion for others. As we open to spirit through the chakras our divine gifts and blessings, in the form of personal qualities, become evident to us. This knowledge allows us to start honouring our soul purpose for being alive. We begin to shine in the true light of our divinity.

Chakras and corresponding nerve plexuses

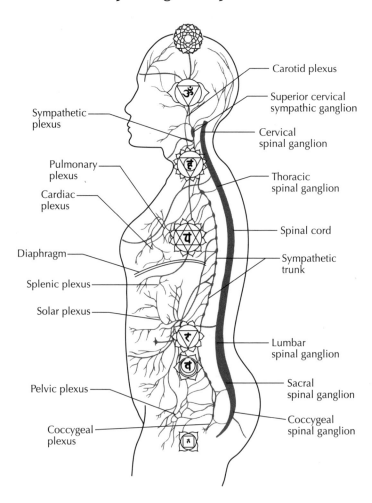

Sympathetic plexus

Pulmonary plexus

Cardiac plexus

Diaphragm

Splenic plexus

Solar plexus

Pelvic plexus

Coccygeal plexus

Carotid plexus

Superior cervical sympathic ganglion

Cervical spinal ganglion

Thoracic spinal ganglion

Spinal cord

Sympathetic trunk

Lumbar spinal ganglion

Sacral spinal ganglion

Coccygeal spinal ganglion

Having looked at how the chakras affect us spiritually and psychologically let us turn to the physical. We know the chakras are located along the central column of the subtle body. The endocrine glands that secrete hormones and the main nerve plexuses, which are concentrations of nerves, lie along the central column of the physical body. They have a close relationship. Subtle energy from the chakras animates these physical structures. Each chakra affects specific nerve plexuses, endocrine glands and body parts. Chakras can therefore be used to strengthen particular parts of the body. It is when the balance of energy flowing through the chakras is disturbed that we eventually suffer dis-ease. If we can maintain a harmonious flow of energy then we can prevent many physical ailments.

The chakras return us to the very core of our being, the control centre, and from here we learn to observe and appreciate the natural laws that govern us. The seven chakras link us with heaven our liberation and earth our limitation. They allow us to experience both: ecstasy and pain. We are free to move our consciousness through the chakras; to perceive our daily lives from any chakra. Each one has a different lesson and we can become stuck in any chakra. With greater application and awareness, we can learn to balance the flow of energy. We can begin to see that what we think of as spirit, mind and body is simply energy manifesting in different densities.

Working With Your Chakras

There are many different levels at which we can work on the chakras. I believe that the chakras are always open and therefore we are already working with them. This openness permits energy to flow in from the universe towards our centre and return to the periphery of our being, and in this way we are kept alive. When the chakras are completely shut down and no longer operational in the body, we move to another plane of existence, where we no longer require a physical vehicle. What is important for us to consider is the degree to which the chakras are open and how much energy is able to flow through them.

Each chakra operates to a varying extent depending on how open it is. Take the heart chakra, for example. It may be that as a child your heart centre was very open and loving came easily to you. At some point you may have experienced rejection or humiliation and as a result of the pain, you closed down your heart chakra, limiting the amount of energy you allow to flow through it. We sometimes hold tight in the chest and abdomen to keep our emotions from flooding out. This reduces energy through the solar plexus and heart centres. Not only do we hold back our pain we also hold back our inner power and capacity to love fully. Working with your chakras helps open them up more fully. This releases blocked energy and restores harmony.

There are numerous reasons why we may choose to work on the chakras and many different ways in which we can work. Working with the chakras is holistic and will influence your entire being. You will find your efforts rewarded with greater spiritual awareness, psycho-emotional development and improved physical health. You will feel more in tune with yourself; more able to cope with the pressures of life. Relaxation will come more easily as you learn to *be* more and do less.

So, What Are Chakras?

Chakras are who you are. They are your very essence. They are wheels of vibrating light that bring inner wisdom and knowledge. Although many such centres exist in your body, there are seven major chakras. Understanding these seven centres and realizing your full potential can provide enough spiritual practice for this life-time. Chakras awaken you to the wealth of spiritual, psychological and physical power you embody. They affect every aspect of your life.

The amount of energy you allow to move through your chakras can readily change as a result of opening to spirit. Throughout time it has been recognized that to obtain more from the universe we need to be ready to receive more. The subtle energy body needs to be cleansed and strengthened through spiritual practice, so you can be whole, happy and live life fully. This book provides some simple techniques for you to begin working on your chakras.

As you work on your chakras the **G**ift **O**f **D**ivinity that dwells at the core of your being will be revealed to you. Your inner rainbow will shine as spiritual blessings are bestowed on you in abundance.

Notes
1   *Arewa, CS* Opening to Spirit, *page 147 (Thorsons, 1998).*

TWO

ENERGY MEDICINE
& Healing

WAY of

Energy Medicine

When we think about medicine, we tend to think of pills and needles, which dominate medical culture in the west today. Western medicine generally focuses on the body or mind. It seldom recognizes the importance of energy and spirit. This has not always been the case. In fact the western way of approaching illness, using medication, is relatively new. It is no older than three or four hundred years. I say new because medicine has a history going back thousands of years in other parts of the world. Even in the west medicine has a history that predates pills and needles.

The word medicine actually means, *'the art and science of preserving health'*. Medicine is broader than pills or injections. The word medicine comes from the Latin 'medicus', doctor, and 'mederi', to heal. 'Med' refers to the middle, as in median or mediate. It is something that intervenes between health and illness, between ease and dis-ease. *Energy medicine is therefore the use of energy to maintain health and alleviate dis-ease.*

When we look at how the ancients viewed medicine we see that they were not limited to working on the physical body. They recognized that we are not merely physical beings. The ancients saw that we are made up of many levels of consciousness. They developed sciences that detail many different levels of the human being. They were then able to apply their medical art to maintaining health and alleviating dis-ease in any of the different levels or bodies.

In my work I identify seven bodies that make up the human organism.[1] These are drawn from the ancient wisdom of Egypt and India. These three-dimensional energy bodies all resonate at different frequencies; some are subtle while others are dense. These bodies are vehicles of the soul. They function in diverse ways to provide us with the experience of being human. They connect us to the universe and the celestial realms. It is through these bodies that we are given the potential to experience altered states of consciousness.

The Aura: Vehicles of the soul

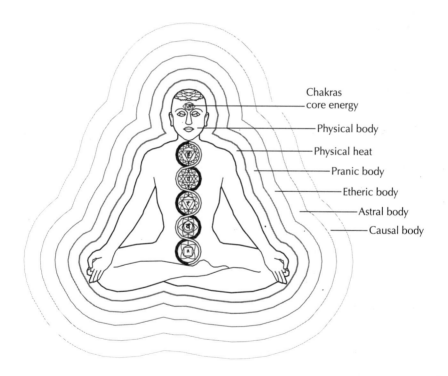

Chakras
core energy
Physical body
Physical heat
Pranic body
Etheric body
Astral body
Causal body

Each body differs in vibration and projection, creating a series of layers that extend beyond the physical body. This extension we call the aura. The layers resonate with specific chakras and correspond to the elements and colours of the rainbow. The energy bodies respond to healing in different ways. The ancients used Energy medicine to heal the different layers. As our spiritual awareness grows and we return to the ways of old, using energy to maintain health and alleviate dis-ease is fast becoming a first choice for healing. Energy medicine is set to regain its power and become the leading method of healing in the twenty-first century.[2]

Vehicles of the Soul

Layer	Body	Aura colour
7	Causal	Purple, white, gold
6	Astral	Indigo, black
5	Etheric	Blue
4	Pranic	Green, rose pink
3	Physical heat	Yellow
2	Physical	Orange
1	Core energy	Red, brown

Healing Methods

The ancients never lacked appreciation for the cosmic relationship that exists between the creator and the created, and between the earth and those that roam upon her back. Maps of the movement of energy, through and around the body were created. The unity between all things did not escape the knowledge of the ancient ones, who left us a rich legacy that we are only just beginning to fully value. Emotions, breath, food, sound and visualization all had a place in the healing traditions of the blessed ancient ones. They utilized their vast knowledge and understanding of natural law in everything they did including medicine.

Element	Healing through	Chakra
Pure spirit	Vibrational energy	Crown
Light	Visualization	Third Eye
Ether	Sound, prayer, ancestors, spirit guides	Throat
Air	Breath, thought power	Heart
Fire	Spiritual healing	Solar Plexus
Water	Physical medicine	Sacral
Earth	Vibrational energy	Root

Healers and shamans from the earliest of times have used energy to cure dis-ease. They have used techniques that are so effective that they have remained in use for thousands of years. Today many ancient healing practices are enjoying renewed popularity. Not surprisingly two of the most favoured methods of energy medicine in the West are homoeopathy and acupuncture. Why? Because they work with the dominant medical culture of pills and needles.

Take a look at the table on page 22. Here you can see how the different layers relate to healing. For example layer 5, the etheric body, responds to healing through sound. This can be music, prayer or communication with your ancestors or spirit guides. It is sound vibration that affects this layer of the human energy field.

> *If you imagine each layer as a globe of vibrating energy, this is an energy field. Fill this globe with its auric colour. This is the energetic ray that emanates through the field. Visualize the related element, see its movement quality filling the globe, the heavy stillness of earth, the flow of water, the quickness of fire, fluctuations of air, the invisibility of ether. These are the elemental qualities that move through each field. Imagine these fields interwoven, their unique energies flowing together to make a whole. They fit perfectly and beautifully. They are you. A wonderful, vibrant, human being.*

These layers require attention in different ways, just like each child in a family is unique and brings different gifts and blessings to a loving home. Each layer provides us with different qualities, different gifts and blessings. Each child needs loving in its own special way. Each layer needs us to focus on it personally.

Different healing modalities use energy in different ways and allow us to work on the specific layers. Through working on all layers we can begin to recreate balanced energy through the entire system. The most important principle to keep in mind is that all layers are interrelated. Therefore, when we effect change on one layer we will automatically create change on the other layers. This allows us to use healing methods that affect both the personal and universal aspects of us. You have heard the saying 'one person's medicine is another person's poison.' Alternative[3] and complementary medicines[4] treat the person and not the disease. They both come under the heading of holistic health care. They work to harmonize physical, emotional, psychological, spiritual and, where possible, social conditions that cause ill health. The focus is always on the underlying cause of the dis-ease and this inevitably involves disturbance to the flow of energy. Holistic health care by its very nature works on all layers of the vibrational energy field and the chakras.

The vibrational energy field and the chakras are central to energy medicine and healing. They are known of and used in many natural therapies. They are often used to aid the diagnostic process and can be cleansed and balanced as part of the corrective treatment.

Energy flows through and around the whole system that we call the body. Different therapies affect different chakras and specific levels of our energy field. Here are some examples.

Colour Therapy

Colour therapy recognizes the important role colour plays in our lives. The main colours used in colour therapy are the rays of the rainbow. These rays relate directly to the chakras and affect how we feel. We talk of 'feeling blue' and 'seeing red'. We choose particular colours to wear each day and to decorate our environments. These colours affect our moods and emotions. They resonate at different levels of our energy field and with awareness we can learn to raise our vibrations and revitalize our energies. Through using colour consciously we can bring balance to our energy field and the chakras. For the specific colours that affect the chakras see chapters 5 to 11.

Crystal Healing

For thousands of years crystals and gems, that come from the earth – our mother, have been used for healing. The ancient Egyptians used them and they continue to be used in Ayurvedic medicine, which is the traditional medicine of India. The subtle energetic vibrations of the crystals have powerful healing effects. Again the different crystals affect specific chakras. This often relates to colour. For example carnelian which is orange relates to the sacral chakra. For specific crystals that affect the chakras see chapters 5 to 11.

Essential Oils

Essential oils can also be used subtly as vibrational medicine. The energetic qualities of flowers, trees, fruits, herbs and grasses have been used as healing remedies for millennia. Essential oils are not actually oil, instead they are thought to be the very life force of the plant captured in its aroma. Essential oils are another example of a treatment that can be used to affect all levels and all chakras. The various oils function very distinctly. Tree oils, such as cypress and sandalwood, are rich oils that affect the root chakra, while lavender works on the crown chakra. See chapters 5 to 11 for specific essential oils that affect the chakras.

Flower Essences

Flower and tree essences contain no more than an energetic imprint of the flower or plant they are made from. They appear to have no real active ingredient, yet they have powerful healing qualities. It is said that they realign the soul and the personality. When personality strays from the 'soul purpose' of this incarnation harmony is lost and ill health and dis-ease will follow. The remedies work well at preventing illness by re-aligning the causal, etheric and physical levels of the vibrational energy field.

Meditation

Meditation has become a buzzword and all kind of activities fall under its umbrella. Visualization is relaxing and beneficial but it is not meditation. True meditation, which is the total stilling of the mind, is extremely difficult. It takes many years of practice to meditate and even then you may simply be concentrating. Learning to totally still the mind and be silent, through yogic practices, gives us the power to realign the entire energy field.

Pranayama

Prana means energy and relates to the life-force that flows through each breath. Yama means control. A simple translation of pranayama is control of the breath. Pranayama, which comes from yoga, provides many breathing techniques designed to purify and realign the pranic layer. Proper breathing is a fundamental aspect of holistic health care. As well as working on the pranic layer it also has a positive effect on the solar plexus and heart chakras.

Purification

Cleansing and purification are important aspects of energy medicine. Cleansing can be done on different levels. We can cleanse on a physical, psycho-emotional or spiritual level. Fasting, positive thinking and meditation all facilitate the movement of energy and create healing. Purification directly affects the etheric level and the throat chakra. Cleansing can also be used to work on a specific chakra or energy body. For example pranayama works on the pranic level.

Ritual

Like meditation, ritual is sometimes misunderstood. Ritual is active spiritual practice. Through ritual we communicate with the universal forces that govern us. Energy is charged and regeneration can take place on all levels. Specific rituals can be used to create healing on various levels; for example a fire ritual can purify the mind and bring richness and clarity to your thoughts and direction in life. Your chosen daily spiritual practice is a ritual that can bring healing and transformation to your life.

Somatic Therapies

Somatic therapies, as the name suggests, work on the physical body. Therapeutic touch is used to restore and maintain health. Therapies such as Polarity Therapy and Shiatsu use touch, energy exercises, diet and positive thinking to create change at all levels of the energy body. The practitioner helps the client to balance the flow of energy through the nadis and meridians.

Sound

Sound is a very powerful healer. Some of the ancient sacred rituals that use sound are now enjoying an increase in popularity. The beating of a drum, the sound of a soothing mantra, words spoken in prayer, all resonate through the throat chakra and the etheric body. We can play relaxing music and be still or feel the rhythm and dance. Music heals, and we are all familiar with its energetic vibrations and uplifting qualities. Music can literally raise the spirit into the higher universal chakras.

Visualization

Vision is the domain of the astral level and the third eye. We can have visions that heal on a physical level. Some visions provide direction in our lives. Dreams, conscious visualizations, imagination, all have the power to create energetic change. We know that if we imagine something bad will happen to us, we create fear. The fear may cause us to sweat, get butterflies in the belly, increase our use of the toilet, stop eating and stop sleeping, the list is endless. The power of the mind is great. We can of course reverse the process and use our imagination to create positive physical reactions that bring healing to the body.

Yoga

Yoga offers a broad theory and many techniques for working on the different vehicles of the soul. Hatha yoga, which is the yoga exercise most people are familiar with, works primarily on the physical level; but of course has a profound effect on all other levels.

These are just some of the healing modalities that affect the chakras and the different energy bodies. Chakras lie at the core of many healing methods. They are central to energy medicine, because they are generators and store houses of energy. As energy flows into the body from the primary source of energy it is stepped down and works on one layer after another. Dis-ease follows the same path; it begins in the energetic system that animates the physical body. Healing therefore must adopt the same route and start with the cause of illness, which is always a disturbance in the flow of energy.

The Healing Process

The process of healing and maintaining health is simple when we understand the movement of energy and the primary role it plays in our lives.

Take a look at the diagram opposite. In it you will see how energy moves from the Divine level at the top to the physical level at the bottom. The universal Ba is the primary source of energy, it is God the creator, the divine life force. You may have your own way of describing this level, but I am sure we can agree that it is the beginning of all things.

As energy steps down from the divine life force the chakras are brought into being. Chakras are generators of energy. They take the primary energy, process it and create a secondary force, that gives rise to the next level within us which is that of the Ka – the animated spirit. It is the level where elements and deities resonate within us. Energy continues to step down and courses through the pathways we call nadis or meridians.

Directional flow of energy

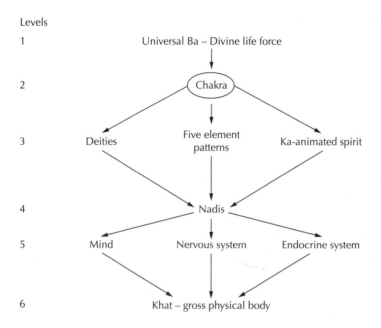

From the nadis energy manifests as individual mind, the nervous system and the endocrine system. At this level energy is moving from mind which is very subtle, to the endocrine system, which is more gross. We can measure the endocrine glands by the hormones they produce. We cannot detect mind, yet we know of its existence because of its action. My yoga teacher, Swami Vishnudevananda used to say. *'We cannot find mind, doctors cannot do a mindectomy.'* They do not know where mind actually is and therefore they cannot remove it. I believe the mind is subtly residing in every cell of the body. I don't think it is restricted to the brain. I think it pervades the whole body, bringing a unique intelligence to the stomach, the hands, the eyes, etc.

We can see that the life-force has stepped down and become physically manifest. This final layer is the Khat – the physical body. What is important to recognize is that illness begins with a disturbance to the flow of energy at the chakra level. This disturbance follows the route from chakra to subtle vehicles (deities, elements and animated spirit) to nadis, to gross vehicles (mind, nervous system and endocrine system) and then becomes a physical ailment.

We can interact at any of the levels. If we can maintain health and harmony within the chakras, then as energy steps down it will flow healthily. We can learn to work spiritually with deities and elements. We can work to maintain the flow of energy through the energy pathways. We can create change psychologically with positive thinking, which has a very powerful effect on the nervous system and the endocrine glands. Or we can take remedies that affect the physical body energetically. Healing can take place on any level and because they are all three dimensional and interrelated, they have an immediate effect on each other.

Lasting healing begins when we connect fully with our **G**ift **O**f **D**ivinity – the chakras. Perhaps I should take a moment to explain that healing does not always mean that you will be without illness or even that this life will not be terminated at what seems like a premature time. No, healing means to be whole, living the life you have to its fullest. This is health. It is possible for people to die and leave the earth plane healed and for people to continue living who are not healed. Think about it for a moment. Healing ourselves is always a choice we can make.

Notes

1   *For detailed information on the aura and the three-dimensional energy bodies, see* Opening to Spirit, *chapter two (Thorsons, 1998).*

2   *It is the twenty-first century on the Gregorian calendar. Other calendars pre-date it by thousands of years.*

3   *Alternative medicine is the name given to natural medicines that can be used as alternatives to orthodox treatments. The five recognized alternative treatments are: acupuncture, chiropractic treatment, herbal medicine, homoeopathy and osteopathy.*

4   *Complementary therapies are natural treatments that can be used alongside orthodox medicine to enhance healing.*

THREE

MULTI-CULTURAL HISTORY

of the Chakras

Ancient Wisdom

Chakras have become popular over the last ten years. More and more people are curious to know what they are and how to use them. People are asking questions and receiving a myriad of answers. The chakras are complex and there is no simple answer to the questions asked. It is important for us to realize that the chakras are not new. They do not belong to a new age move-ment. In fact the only thing that can be termed *new age* is the growing awareness of and demand for knowledge of the ancient traditions. The increase in spiritual curiosity is new. It is a good thing. It feels as if we have come full circle. We are now return-ing to the ways of old. We are desperately seeking that which was lost. When I look around me I see spirit re-appearing in many forms. We are experiencing emptiness and our spiritual hunger must be satisfied. But as with all food eaten after a period of fast-ing, we must take special care. It is good to know the source of the food, take time with its preparation. Chew each mouthful slowly and thoroughly. If it does not taste good, spit it out. Fast foods and processed foods may be quicker, but can they really provide the nourishment you seek? Before your belly is too full, rest and allow your soul food to be digested. The chakras have a very long history, and as you read this chapter you will become familiar with their source.

There has never been a time in the history of the human race when spiritual energy has not been important. From the time the first humans began walking upon mother Africa's back we have held awe and respect for spirit. We have recognized that which is greater than ourselves. We have acknowledged that which can create or destroy us. We have named the energies. We have both loved them and feared them. Thanks and praises have been shouted, sung and whispered to the invisible forces that shape our lives. Spiritual practice goes back as far as the human race itself.

When we look closely at the chakras we see that they combine many levels of spiritual knowledge. We say that a picture paints a thousand words. Images contain so much information. The chakras use symbols and images to contain hidden wisdom. Through using images a whole wealth of knowledge can be conveyed. Traditionally the initiated would meditate on the chakras either by painting them and then viewing them externally or by internally visualizing them. The geometric shapes depicting the chakras are known as yantras. Yantras are divine symbols that hold the power of the divine. They are used to help us bring the vastness of the universe into our conscious awareness. The unfathomable mystery of life is made available by meditating on the chakra images.

Because the universe is so immense the ancients devised ways of capturing this vastness in symbols. Each chakra image holds within it the boundless reality of the universe. In this book I have used simplified diagrams of the chakras. When you work carefully with them you will begin to experience some of the expansiveness they portray.

Chakras have many aspects depicted within them. They are shaped like lotus flowers, and each chakra has a differing number of petals. The root has four, the sacral has six, and so on. (See the images opening chapters 5 to 11.) The petals represent the frequency of energy emanating from a particular centre. In detailed images of the chakras, colours, symbols, elements, mantras, deities and animals are all represented within each individual chakra. All these different images tell us something about the universal energy that moves through us via the chakras. The animal associated with the heart chakra, for example, is the gazelle. This is an animal that moves with grace, it is light and runs swiftly through the air. This tells us that the heart energy is light and graceful, it is gentle and fast moving. We actually use the word dear to refer to someone we love or as a means of respect. Everything else originally depicted in the chakra images also has a depth of meaning. They help us understand the body we live in and the earth we live on. They teach us about the laws of the universe that we live under and the divine spirit that we live with.

I am trying in words to create a picture of all that the chakras are. It is a challenge, and I feel I may be beginning to confuse you. This is the very reason why the ancients used images to convey the message, and why they went inside and meditated on internal stillness and silence. This way they could really begin to understand the universal reality I am trying to write about. You might want to do the same. It is perfectly all right to skip through the early chapters and scan the rest of the book. Look at the chapters that centre on the chakras. I am sure you will find a practice that resonates with you. Take some time to meditate. This way your own unique chakras will begin to reveal themselves to you. Return to the beginning of the book later.

If you have made a detour I hope you have enjoyed it. I am sure you will now have a better feeling sense of your chakras and what they represent. We are continuing now to explore the history of some of the different aspects of the chakras.

The Elements

It is only when we examine the make up of the chakras that we can really see their long history. Each chakra is associated with an element. The ancients lived at the mercy of the elements and were very familiar with the overwhelming force they imposed on their existence. They had to learn to understand the elements in order to survive. Energy has the power to both create and destroy; this they saw in nature. Storms destroy while the sun creates. The elemental rhythms of nature bring creation, growth and destruction. For this reason, the ancients saw the elements as worthy of respect. Our earliest Ancestors honoured the earth, sun, wind, water and even the space[1] in which we all reside.

A close relationship with the elements and nature made people aware of the forces within the body as well as surrounding them. It became evident to our ancestors that the same forces that surround us also move through us. *'As above so below'* is the well-known Egyptian teaching. The very elements we see in nature are found inside us. Winds, for example, scatter seeds, playing a part in all creation; they can move with great speed, but they also have an illusive nature. The ancients began to liken the mind to the character of the wind – creative, forever changing and illusive. Over thousands of years, a complex system developed which relates the elements to human experience. Part of this legacy remains in commonplace metaphors. Referring to someone as 'full of hot air', a 'bit wet' or 'too fiery', are expressions we all understand today. This may have been considered primitive, but it is, in fact, ancient physics.

The Number Seven

There are seven chakras. This is a spiritually rich number. Seven has a long history of spiritual significance. Again I would say it goes back to the very beginning of time in Africa. Ancient Africans, such as the Egyptians, observed the number seven appearing naturally in the universe. They saw seven in the sky above, in the stars we call the Pleiades or the Seven Sisters. They saw seven uplifting colours of the rainbow that we can still see when a rainy day turns sunny. The importance of the number seven has travelled with the migration of people around the globe. Seven now occurs in spiritual traditions in many diverse cultures.

We create music using seven notes of the musical scale. Our week is divided into seven days that stretch from the day of the sun to that of Saturn. The Christian creation myth centres around seven days. It took six days to create the world, and the seventh day, which corresponds to the crown chakra, was declared a day of rest and oneness with our creator. The Bible has many references to the number seven.

Many more sevens are to be found in our diverse cultures. I have introduced a few, but you probably know of some more. You can see that seven is a powerful organizing principle. It is a number of fullness and completion. Seven is a creative number that produces order.

Serpents

The snake is another powerful symbol used in spirituality. It is a symbol of both good and evil. It represents the balance of opposites; the yin and yang of all creation.

Chakras and Snakes

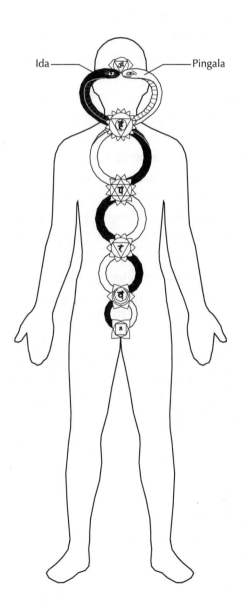

Ida — — Pingala

When we look at a diagram of all the chakras we see they are depicted in a column, one on top of the other. The root is at the bottom and the crown at the top. Also ascending from the bottom to the top are two lines, one dark and one light. These two pathways are known as Nekhebet and Uatchet or ida and pingala, negative and positive energy respectively. They are sometimes shown as two entwined serpents whose heads meet at the third eye. They represent duality. This is our everyday reality. The fluctuations we make between happy and sad, glad or mad, empty or full. Duality is night and day, hot and cold, woman and man. It is when we can transcend beyond duality, to a place above the third eye chakra, that we come to the centre of oneness at the crown chakra. The snake is found in the spiritual traditions and mythologies of most cultures. The snake was thought to have everlasting life because it sheds its skin and was seen to be reborn. The Egyptians had the winged serpent goddess, a protector of the pharaohs. The Chinese have the mystical dragon, a combination of the snake and a bird. The snake appears many times in the Bible. It is a symbol of feminine wisdom and masculine power. Are you beginning to get the picture of how all these overlapping aspects are present within the chakras? This is only a brief overview. For more details, see my first book, *Opening to Spirit*, where much of the above is explained in greater detail.

Buto – the winged serpent Goddess

WAY of

Cultural Time Line

We know that the symbols and all the spiritual wisdom they contain have been with us since the beginning of time. Let us now take a look at the chakras and their various aspects, as they have been presented in diverse cultures through the ages.

Africa

Tanzania is the birthplace of the human race. This is the place where people first roamed the earth. It is in this mountainous region of Central Africa that we find Mount Meru. Meru is the sacred mountain of love; its name means all things surrounding love. Meru appears in the mythology of the ancient Egyptians and the Indians. Both peoples had extensive spiritual traditions that have survived until today. Knowledge of the chakras is found in both traditions. In India the name given to the spine and the chakras is Merudanda. This sacred mountain represents life's journey from the bottom of the mountain to the top, from the root chakra to the crown. It also represents the original journey from the mountaintop to its base on earth. It is believed that we come from the Gods, who reside at the top of Mount Meru. As the cradle of humanity this sacred mountain is the original place where knowledge of the energy systems and the chakras began.

People travelled north from central Africa and populated Egypt. It is from the ancient Egyptians that we get the symbol of the caduceus. This ancient symbol has been used throughout time to symbolize energy and the chakras. We can still see its significance today in the medical and pharmaceutical professions, where the image continues to symbolize healing. It shows the twin snakes, ida and pingala, or the ureaus, Nekhebet and Uatchet, as they were known to the Egyptians. A chakra is formed at each point where the snakes cross. In the middle of the diagram you can see a central column: this is the shushumna or the staff of Hermes. The Greek deity Hermes comes directly from the Egyptian God scribe and wisdom teacher Dheuti, known to the Greeks as Thoth. The shushumna is the neutral centre where we want to encourage energy to flow. When energy is free to move up the shushumna, through each of the chakras, we experience a peace and bliss beyond explanation.

The ancient Egyptians also used the scale of Maat to measure how much an individual had progressed spiritually. Maat is the Goddess of truth and justice, and her scales continue to be seen in law courts to this day. Each measure on the scale represents a different level of consciousness, as do the chakras. In ancient times people were held responsible for their spiritual evolution. People were expected to rise up and develop the divine potential of human nature. Various techniques were used to awaken spiritual power, such as ritual, meditation and hekau – sacred words and mantras. This is the same process used to awaken the chakras and uplift the dormant spiritual energy that moves through us. The ancient Egyptians influenced a lot of the Indian yogic system, which is the main source of knowledge on the chakras. There are many similarities between the two spiritual systems. This is also due to the Ethiopian origins of both the Ancient Egyptians and the Ancient Indians.

The Rainbow – Australia, Nigeria and Ireland

The original Australians have a very long history of working with subtle energy. Wawalu, the rainbow serpent, is the carrier of the life-force. Here again we see commonalities. Wherever we find the rainbow in spiritual traditions it usually relates to the chakras. The ancients observed that the arc of the rainbow comes from the

45

heavens and can be seen to reach down and touch the earth. To our ancestors the rainbow was like a ladder between heaven and earth. And of course the chakras are our own inner ladder connecting us to both heaven – the crown chakra, and earth – the root chakra. Rainbows are found in diverse mythologies yet the spiritual message seems to be the same. Òṣumaré is the rainbow serpent of the Yoruba Spiritual Tradition from Nigeria. Òṣumaré unites opposites, blending masculine and feminine energies. She can be seen swallowing her own tail, creating a circle that symbolizes eternity. This union delivers a message of lasting peace and harmony. In Irish mythology it is said that there is a pot of gold at the end of the rainbow. This is symbolic of the journey through the chakras. This saying teaches that spiritual ascension, up the rainbow or through the chakras, will lead us to the priceless golden gift of enlightenment.

Native America, Peru

Despite the destruction of Native American cultures, the original Americans have maintained rich earth-based spiritual traditions. Many of these traditions have teachings on the chakras. Rosalyn Bruyere, in her book *Wheels of Light*, says:

> *The native peoples have an attitude that all the chakra centers are good, valid and important. These people, who, by their own accounts, have lived here [USA] for fifteen thousand years, have had a working knowledge of the body's energy system since that time. They also have maintained a tradition of practices, rituals and ceremonies that affect those energy centers.*

Inca shamans from Peru continue to heal using the energy of the chakras. They work with eight main chakras. The additional one is above the crown. Each centre has a powerful energy, many relating to power animals. In Inca shamanism the root chakra is the home of the serpent Goddess, Sachamama. Navajo medicine men and women also heal using the energy centres and the aura.

India

Although knowledge of the chakras goes back to the beginning of time and appears universal, it is from the Indian Tantra yoga tradition that we get the majority of our current teachings. Understanding of the chakra system has been highly developed in India, which is one of the few places on earth where spiritual tradition has remained largely unchanged for many thousands of years. Tantra yoga is one of the spiritual paths of the Dravidian people who are descendants of Ethiopia. Tantra includes amongst its teachings the chakras, astronomy, astrology, kundalini, hatha yoga, and the worship of the Goddesses Shakti and Durga and the Gods Shiva and Vishnu. This book is strongly influenced by the ancient yoga practice and philosophy, which I have studied for many years.

China

China has a very sophisticated tradition of energy medicine. This focuses on a number of energy pathways called meridians. The meridians relate to different organs. The elements play a major role in Chinese healing systems. These elements, however, differ from the ones relating to the chakras. The major chakras are not directly seen on the energy maps used in Chinese medicine, which were also adapted by the Japanese. But it is thought by some that the tsubos or acupuncture points relate to some of the minor and miniscule chakras of the body. Some practitioners of Chinese medicine do superimpose the chakra system and use it alongside other diagnostic systems.

Middle East

Some religions have mystic traditions closely associated with them. The Sufi mystic tradition is closely associated with Islam and the kaballah relates to the Judaic religion. When we examine the kaballah we see that it depicts a tree of life with seven levels of evolving consciousness. Study of this spiritual system takes the aspirant on a journey of self-discovery leading from earth to heaven. The lessons that are taught along the way are similar to those that awaken the chakras. Within Sufism the soul is thought to pass through seven ascending levels of consciousness. These are known as maqām or stations of the soul. The soul journeys from the first level, which is a place of egoism and preoccupation with self, to union with the divine, which is the final resting-place of the soul. Yet again we witness the familiar evolutionary process, the movement from ordinary consciousness to Divine consciousness.

Europe

The earth-based spiritual traditions of pre-Christian Europe recognized many aspects of the chakras. The elements were widely understood and used in healing. The serpent had power associated with it and seven was a spiritually-charged number. In Glastonbury, a powerful spiritual centre in England, there is an earth mound known as Glastonbury Tor. This mound is an ancient sacred site, where Pagans would gather under the moon and circumambulate the tor in seven ascending circles, until in ecstasy they reached the top. Similar ascension rituals have been reclaimed today and symbolize the spiritual journey through the chakras.

The mystery traditions of Egypt and India travelled to Europe in the early twentieth century bringing knowledge of the chakra system with them. A number of Europeans took an interest in the mysteries and rapidly spread their teachings. The Theosophists, led by Madame Blavatsky, Annie Besant and the Reverend Charles Leadbeater, published writings on Egyptian Spirituality, Hermeticism, Yoga and traditions of the East. Jung also wrote on eastern philosophy, particularly mandalas. Their work is still recognized today. The Reverend Leadbeater was clairvoyant and he recorded his own visions of the aura and chakras.

Russia

Kirlian photography, developed in 1940s Russia by Semyon and Valentina Kirlian allowed many people to see the aura. It is now possible to consistently photograph the electromagnetic field that surrounds the body. People have been able to view pictures of the aura around their hands. This method provides the objective evidence many people seek.

USA

In more recent times several research studies have been carried out on the chakra system. During the 1970s a healer named Rosalyn Bruyere, and a scientist, Dr Valerie Hunt, conducted an eight-year research project on the human electromagnetic field.[2] They were able to verify the colours of the chakras and the aura. Rosalyn Bruyere was able to see the colours that Dr Hunt measured with electrical instruments. Emissions of the energy field and how they change in relation to emotions were also recorded in this particular study.

To Conclude

From this brief cultural history we see that the chakras are known in many parts of the world. They are vehicles of consciousness, measures of spiritual evolution, stepping stones on the journey towards enlightenment. They are found in the secret mystery traditions of ancient cultures. Their purpose is to lift our souls, to awaken us and return us to divine union with our creator. As knowledge of the chakras becomes unveiled and loses some of its secrecy and mystery, it is essential that we do not undermine, and also lose, the depth and potency of the chakras.

As awareness of the chakras grows we are seeing all kinds of chakra-related paraphernalia. Computer-generated programmes claim to read your chakras and locate energy blockages. Items of jewellery are thought to keep your chakras spinning. Music tapes and oils designed to relax, open and balance your chakras can be found in abundance. According to some teachers, new chakras are being born as you read. Yes, the chakras really are becoming very popular. We can work with the chakras at different levels, from superficial to in-depth. It is useful to be able to distinguish the difference. It is important for us to remember, as I said at the beginning of this chapter, the chakras are not new, they are ancient. And, therefore, it is likely to be the ancient techniques, ones that have stood the test of time, that will serve us best in working to develop our spiritual consciousness. Meditation, ritual, prayer and chanting are all powerful time-tested ways of deeply evolving our consciousness. As we reconnect with our lost souls, let us not forget the wisdom ways of our ancestors.

Notes

1   *This space is known as Ether and is the element that relates to the throat chakra.*

2   *Bruyere, Rosalyn,* Wheels of Light, *Simon and Schuster, 1994.*

FOUR

PREPARING TO WORK

with your Chakras

Energy flows through and around you at all times and you are affected by this energy. If your intention is to work with your chakras, then you will need to begin by increasing your awareness of your internal and external environment. This chapter explains how to make the space around you conducive to chakra work and how to create an internal environment that will accommodate an increased flow of energy.

Sacred Space

Space is one of the things we can always use more of. But how do we use the space that we have? Do you have sacred space in your home? A place where you can go and be alone, a quiet place where you can relax and rejuvenate the innermost parts of yourself. We can all use sacred space. You will find your journey through the chakras is smoother if you prepare beforehand.

Sacred space was important to our ancestors. They created sacred space in their villages, towns and cities. They had sacred space in their homes and they learned to transform their physical bodies into temples where energy was free to flow. Sacred space is an environment where the energy has been cleansed and uplifted. The vibration is high and whenever you go to this place your own energy is raised.

When we are working with chakras and the energy field it becomes important to have sacred space in which to work, relax, or just be. Creating sacred space enhances all the work we do. Before commencing work on the chakras it is good to create sacred space externally and internally.

Our external environments mirror our internal environments. If your home is untidy and cluttered the chances are your mind is confused and cluttered. When you begin to sort out your living space, your mind will also take on a new sense of clarity. By clearing your surroundings you can begin to clear your mind. A clear mind creates space for the sacred to enter. Try it, it works.

Creating Sacred Space

Creating sacred space is done in two stages. The first stage is cleansing; this is both physical and energetic cleansing. The space needs to be clean and free of negative vibrations. You may wish to cleanse your entire home or just the room you are going to use for spiritual practice. Secondly, the energy in the space needs to be raised and this can be done by clearing away clutter and creating an altar. You can place items on your altar that will raise energy and make the space sacred for you.

Once your space has been cleansed physically it is ready for energetic cleansing. Unseen and unwelcome energies can accumulate in our homes. Like dust, negative energy gathers in the corners. There are lots of ways to remove negative energy from your home. I have listed the main tools used for clearing energy according to the elements.

Earth Crystals can be pointed into the corners of rooms to absorb energy. *Amber* purifies and reduces negative energy. *Amethyst* raises vibrations.

Water Two or three drops of *Frankincense* in water can be sprayed into room corners and up to the ceiling. A fine mist of

55

water will energetically cleanse the room.

Fire and Air A *sage smudge stick* that has been set alight, and left softly smoking (put out any flames), can be wafted around the room, especially into corners where negative energy accumulates. Alternatively incense can be used. The smoke cleanses the space, and is thought to carry our prayers up to the Gods.

Ether Sound is a great transformer of energy. *Hands* can be clapped, *bells* rung, *chimes* tinkled, *drums* beaten or *Tibetan bowls* played. All will clear negative energy.

Negative energy may also have accumulated in your home in the form of clutter. You may want to have a serious clear out. Anything in the way goes. If it doesn't serve you, i.e. you don't use it, wear it or love it, let it go and create space for the sacred. Yes, emptiness = space = ether energy, which is filled with the Divine. Space is Divine. Once you have created space you can begin preparing your altar.

Altar Building

An altar is a visual representation of the sacred. They are spaces where the physical and spiritual worlds meet. We can all create and use altars regardless of our spiritual, religious or philosophical beliefs. An altar is a way of connecting with nature. An altar brings the beauty and mystery of nature to our attention at all times; whether we are just soaking in the energy of our altar or using it for spiritual practice. Altars are simple yet profound ways of honouring the sacred, which many of us feel called to do, but often we just don't know how. Living in the modern world can alienate us from

the sacred.

Choosing consciously to build an altar will raise the vibration of your home. An altar can be used to develop your focus on different aspects of your life. A client of mine, while pregnant, asked me to spiritually cleanse her home. She wanted to clear any negative energy and prepare the space into which her new child would be welcomed. Together we cleansed the space, chanted and prayed. An altar was then created for the baby. Gifts were placed on it, books, crystals, a candle, photographs and special items to symbolize the desired intellectual and spiritual development of the child. The altar will grow with the child. As the parents use the altar the child will become familiar with its sacred purpose. As the child grows this will become her special place, a sacred space where the child will learn to honour the sacred. This is a very beautiful way to energetically manifest intention.

After your space has been cleansed physically and energetically and all the clutter has been cleared you can begin to build your altar. Think about the spiritual energy that you want to create. A carefully prepared altar will have a powerful magnetic field around it that will charge and uplift the items placed on it and the people who go near it. Decide where your altar is going to be. Preferably it will be in the same place where you do your spiritual practice. Can it take over a spare room, or a corner in a room? Can you use a shelf or tabletop? Use whatever space you have. Then take a look around your home: you are likely to find some of the items you need for your altar. Choose something to represent each of the elements, earth, water, fire, air and ether. For example, crystals, a chalice of fresh spring water, a beautiful candle, incense for the air element and a bell, drum or singing bowl to represent ether, which is the element of sound. What you do not already have, collect from Mother Nature, and remember to give thanks to her for everything she offers you. Anything else that you need, enjoy buying. As you buy your sacred items, have an appreciation for the richness they will bring to your environment and, ultimately, your spirit. Arrange a cloth on your altar and then position all your items. This forms the basis of your altar, which you can then personalize with photographs, your favourite flowers and items that you find spiritually uplifting.

> *When you have finished, light your candle, sit*
> *in front of your altar and say a prayer of thanks.*
> *Ask for any guidance you need and make your*
> *intentions known, so you can be assisted in your*
> *growth. Take a moment just to breathe and be still.*

Take special care of your altar and it will serve you well.

Your sacred space is now complete and the external preparations are taken care of. It is now time to turn your attention to your internal environment. Internal cleansing is very important for chakra work. Before the ancients did any energy work they would fast and cleanse the energy pathways. If you are to increase the flow of energy through your system then you need to prepare the route. If you are expecting an increase in traffic you need clear roads.

Internal Purification

There are many ways to cleanse the system. Perhaps the most effective is fasting. This is also the one most people are afraid of. We think it will be very difficult to fast. We fear we will get hungry, tired and run down. Think about it, our souls are already hungry, we are already tired, for some of us exhausted would be the appropriate word, and we are already run down. Our systems are congested energetically. So we have little to fear. Fasting will in fact feed the soul and bring a much-needed rest to the digestive system and all other parts of your body. Fasting rids the body of toxins and helps to regulate the internal organs. It also helps clear the mind and raise the spirits. Often we will feel energized after a period of fasting. As far as the chakras are concerned the main reason for fasting is to purify the nadis – energy pathways. This facilitates the flow of energy through and around the body, which is the ultimate purpose of chakra work.

Caution: Fasting is perfectly safe for most people, but it is recommended that you check with a doctor or natural health practitioner if you suffer from any diagnosed illness or take prescribed medication.

One-day Fast

The evening before your fast, eat a light nutritious meal, low in sugars (sugar tends to create food craving). On the day of your fast, drink at least four litres of pure spring water that has been kept at room temperature. If you can drink more, that is fine. The idea is to completely flush out the alimentary canal, the liver and the kidneys. Pure water, unlike other liquids, moves straight through the body, flushing out toxins as it proceeds. Eventually your urine will be clear and you will feel light. When I fast for a day, providing I am mentally prepared, I do not feel hungry. The following day, break your fast with fruit, steamed vegetables and other light foods. This fast is good to do one day a month.

For more detailed information on different types of fasting and guidelines for longer fasts see *Opening to Spirit*.

Breathing

One of the main carriers of energy is the breath. Breathing is vital to energy work and especially chakra work. Prana, chi, shekem and àṣẹ are names given to the life force that animates us. This force moves through the breath. The Latin source of the word 'respiration' is 'spiritus'. Thus we see in our language the link between breath and the spirit that moves us. When we hear creation myths from many cultures we learn that we are moulded from our mother the earth and it is our father from above that blows life into us. His breath gives us life. We come alive when prana begins to move through us. We need a high level and good flow of prana moving through and around our systems in order to maintain health.

> *Be aware of your breath right now ...*
> *Is your breath deep, shallow or imperceptible?*
> *Where does your breath reach?*
> *Can you feel it in your toes, fingertips, deep in*
> *your belly, in your head? Let your breath out.*
> *Take a full, deep breath and feel the breath*
> *move through your entire body ...*
> ***Repeat seven times and be aware of how***
> ***you feel different.***

Your life can be completely transformed through learning to breathe properly. Try to incorporate the breathing exercises below into your daily routine.

Three-Part Yogic Breath

Begin by lying on your back, on the floor in the relaxation posture. Let your feet be about eighteen inches apart and falling out to the sides. Place your hands about six inches away from your body with palms facing upwards. Your chin is slightly down towards your chest in order to lengthen the back of your neck. Your eyes should be gently closed and your mouth gently open. Let go of any tightness or tension. Release and relax the whole body. Bring your attention to your breath.

Yogic Breathing

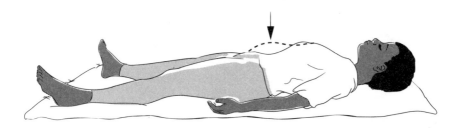

1   *Breathe in fully through your nose,*
     raising your abdomen. Open your chest
     and completely fill your lungs.

2   *Hold your breath comfortably, keeping*
     your body totally still for a count of four.
     (This can be increased with practice.)

3   *Exhale slowly through your nose and*
     empty your lungs completely.
     Feel your abdomen pulling down towards
     the floor. Repeat this three-part breath
     three to seven times.

61

This exercise allows full and correct use of the breathing apparatus. It restores movement to the diaphragm and intercostal muscles. Five times more oxygen flows into your lungs and around your body's cells. This helps flush out toxins. The nervous system relaxes and concentration improves. The ability to control your breath is fundamental to spiritual development.

Caution: People with back problems may wish to lay down with knees raised and feet placed flat on the floor in front of the buttocks.

Cleansing breath

1   *Breathe in fully to a count of three.*
2   *Hold the breath for a count of twelve.*
3   *Breathe out to a count of six.*
     Repeat the above three stages seven times.

This cleansing breath can be done at any time and in any place. It can be used whenever you need to relax and centre your self. Both breathing exercises will help purify your nadis.

If fasting does not appeal to you or you find it difficult to fast at the moment, try to at least work with your breath to cleanse and purify your system in preparation for chakra work. It will enhance any spiritual work you go on to do.

Cleansing your Energy Field

To cleanse your self of negative energy you can use any of the tools mentioned in the section on 'creating sacred space'. Take crystals, a frankincense spray, a smudge stick or a bell and pass it through and around your aura. Work up the front of your body slowly and then down the back of your body finishing at your feet. Ask for all negative energy to be removed and neutralized by the power of our mother the earth. Give thanks.

Time for your Self

Now that you have learnt how to create sacred space, build an altar and perform your personal cleansing, all that is left is for you to declare time and space for your Self. Decide how you will take time for your Self from the twenty-four hours we are blessed with in each and every day. This designated time is just to develop your Self personally and spiritually. Decide whether mornings are better for you or evenings? Do you want to get up half an hour earlier? You need about 20 to 30 minutes a day; the same amount of time it takes some people to put on make-up. Or you may want to begin slowly and work on your chakras once a week. Decide what will work best for you and let anyone you share your home with know that you cannot be disturbed during this time. This is your special time. Explain to children. It is good for young children to see their parents take special time. They learn that it is important to have some time to your Self and they too will honour time for themselves as they get older.

Thought Power

When preparing to work on the chakras it is useful to understand the power of the mind. *'Energy follows thought'* is a well-known saying from the kemitic – ancient Egyptian – texts. The intention we hold will affect the outcome of any work we do. A positive intention will bring positive results. It is also good to maintain an open mind. The outcome from our work may not always be the one we expected. It will, however, be the right one, and we will be called on by our creator to learn the lessons life has in store for us. We need to accept that we are tiny drops of divinity in the ocean of the Divine. From our limited perspective we cannot understand everything. We can merely learn to recognize that everything is going according to plan; the greater plan. We are learning lessons each and every step of the way.

Thoughts and language have power. When we think *we cannot*, or we say *we cannot*, then that is what we create, *we cannot*. It is the choice we have made. We have created the vibration for failure. Therefore, if we want to be successful and achieve our goal of greater spiritual awareness, health, happiness and abundance in our lives we must believe it is available to us. We must feel worthy of richness in the broadest sense of the word. And we must affirm in thought and language to ourselves that we are moving towards our fullness in every step we take.

As you read you are growing in abundance. Right this very minute you are unfolding into the powerful divine person that you truly are. You are answering a calling deep within you to be a better person, a wiser person. You are changing right now, we change all the time. You are developing yourself spiritually and learning new ways of being. As you read and put what you read into practice, be open to accept your self as the wonderful divine being that you are.

As you become acquainted with the chakras and begin to do the exercises suggested in this chapter and those that follow, your energy will gradually change. You will become aware of subtle differences that take place within and around you. You may experience times of heightened pleasure and times of pain. When we enter deeply into ourselves we find both pleasure and pain. Sometimes the pain hits us first because we often bury our capacity for ecstasy under our pain. As we begin to release the tensions that hold back pleasure we start to feel our pain. With the pain lifted, pleasure is then free to rise. It can be beneficial to use a journal to make notes of your experiences and register the changes that occur. A journal can be a great support. You can share your innermost feelings with it and find clarity in times of confusion. Writing in my journal was a healing tool that I found extremely helpful when I first started my spiritual journey. I continue to use a journal now, because it gives form to my thoughts and can clarify things for me. The process of keeping a journal is very powerful; it acts like a friend and a guide.

Closing Down your Energy Field

Please do not underestimate the powerful effects of chakra work. Chakra work is designed to expose you to an increased flow of energy through your system. You may also start to pick up more energy from your environment. If you find your energy is too open and you are becoming overwhelmed, you may be picking up too much from the ether. If this happens to you, ground yourself by returning to root chakra work, work more slowly or stop altogether; your intuition will tell you which. It may be that you need to purify your system more through the breathing exercises mentioned above.

If you want to close your energy field down, *visualize each chakra as a flower head that opens and closes. Begin at the crown and work down to the root. See each flower very gently closing down. All the petals slowly return to the centre. Energy still passes in and out as the flower breathes but the central core is completely protected. Know that with your help, the universe will always keep you safe.*

I hope you have enjoyed preparing for chakra work. I am sure you can already feel the difference in the energy both within and around you. Any time you spend working on your inner self will be richly rewarded. In the following chapters we will explore each chakra in detail.

FIVE

THE ROOT
Chakra

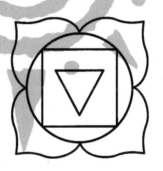

Characteristics of the Root Chakra

Name:	Root, Muladhara
Meaning:	Root, support, foundation
Symbol:	Square
Location:	Perineum
Main function:	Embodiment

Spiritual Characteristics

Colour:	Red
Element:	Earth
Quality:	Grounding
Deities:	**Africa:** Auset (Isis), Geb Sekmet, Odùduwà, Onílé, Asaka
	India: Shakti, Kundalini, Ganesha
	Europe: Gaia, Persephone
	All Earth Goddesses

Physical Characteristics

Gland:	*Adrenals*
Nerve plexus:	*Coccygeal plexus*
Body parts:	*Legs, bones, spine, colon*
Expression:	*Healthy and happy in your physical body*
Disturbance:	*Prone to illness, dislike of your own body*
Physical ailments:	*Lower back pain*
	Haemorrhoids
	Constipation
	Sciatica
	Knee problems
	Obesity and weight problems
	Addictive behaviour (drugs, alcohol, sex, etc.)
	Depression

Psychological Characteristics

Statement: 'I have' (a physical body)
Emotions in balance: Courage; Safe and secure; Sensational, alive; Moved
Emotions unbalanced: Fear; Rigid; Weighed down; Unmoving

Ways to Work

Oils: Patchouli, cypress, vetivert
Gems: Red jasper, garnet, smoky quartz, obsidian, ruby, black star sapphire, red jade

Root – Body

The root chakra is the first of the seven chakras. It is the foundation on which the other chakras sit. It is located between the anus and the genitals on the perineal floor. When we sit for meditation, this chakra is in direct contact with our mother the earth. It is from the earth that this chakra draws energy.

Action is a root chakra word. Completion and actually getting things done depend on a good flow of energy through the root chakra. Earth energy is focused at this centre and earth energy is about manifestation and bringing things into being. If you think about it we are born from the root chakras of our mothers. Not only do we come into the world through the root chakra but everything we wish to create finds completion through root chakra energy. We often have great ideas, which are air energy, we get enthusiastic which is fire energy. We start things that we will never finish unless we can stimulate earth energy and the root chakra; this is because root chakra energy is about grounding things in reality. Sometimes we complete things easily. We ground them with little effort. At other times knowing how to work on the root chakra to help us complete projects will be very useful. Let's take this book: it has passed through the idea stage, reached the writing stage and finally arrived at completion. Energy has flowed freely and the book has been successfully created. This is the process for all things. Root chakra energy has a major role in completion. If you find yourself not starting or finishing projects, energy is not flowing freely through your root chakra. Begin the rebalancing exercises in this chapter.

The root chakra also relates to your physical body and your relationship to it. Your body is a finely structured temple, a temple that houses your divine spirit. Through your body you can learn to feel the movement of energy as it ebbs and flows. Your body can also hold back the flow of energy. When energy is restricted dis-ease will soon follow. A healthy relationship with your root chakra increases health throughout the body. Acknowledging the needs of your body and taking good care of it helps to maintain the root chakra. Eating good wholesome food, getting sufficient sleep, taking enough exercise and good hygiene are some of the essential elements of life that keep the physical body fit and healthy.

Physically the root chakra relates to the denser parts of the body such as the bones and the spine, the legs and the knees. It also relates to red blood cells, and the colon (large intestine). All these body parts correspond to earth energy, which is the densest element. Root chakra-related ailments can occur in any of these body parts. A balanced root chakra improves the health of your whole body.

Root – Mind

Psychologically the root chakra takes care of our direction in life. A square is depicted within the root chakra. To the ancient Egyptians it was the symbol of achievement. The square represents strong foundations and solidity. The four corners symbolize the four directions north, south, east and west. From a strong foundation we can move out in any direction. We simply need to remember our soul purpose for being born. Why are you here? What are the precious gifts you bring to offer the world? Once these questions are confidently answered it is possible to move forward knowing that the universe will support your journey through life.

We are all born for a divine reason and we all have a sacred job to do here on earth. In order to do the work we are destined for, we must discover our unique individual qualities. These are the affinities we have; the skills we have been blessed with. What do you do well? What do you really love doing and excel in? Is that the work you are destined to do? For some of us raising the next generation is the work we are destined to do. Parenting is perhaps the most important contribution we can offer the world, or maybe teaching is your vocation, or one of the caring professions. Communication and sharing are essential roles; this may be done through the arts, music, writing, painting and dancing, which are all wonderful ways of sharing the divine gifts bestowed on us.

It is through working on the root chakra that we can gain access to our unique gifts. It is here that we gain the necessary insight to help us achieve our full potential and be all that we can be.

It is also at the root chakra that we experience fear. The paralysing emotion that holds us back. The emotion that is behind the words *I can't,* or *It's too late,* or *I won't be able to,* or *I will try later,* or *I would if I had time, money, a babysitter,* etc, etc, etc. I need say no more: we all know the many excuses we find, when really we are just too afraid to move forward. So what is the next best thing? Stay stuck and do lots of complaining. We all know the scenario *If only I had ... then I would ... and that would make me feel ....* This is blocked energy in the root chakra. Your full creative potential, gifts and blessings are not allowed to flow. If you can identify with any of the above then you are holding yourself back. Dwelling inside you is everything you need to change your situation. Powerful energy for change is with you all the time. All you have to do is learn to access and use it.

Through working on the chakras we can achieve our goals. Working on the root chakra can transform fear into courage, pain into plea-sure and negative energy into positive life-affirming creative energy.

We can begin by acknowledging that everything is possible as long as it is part of the Creator's plan. With divine assistance we can achieve anything that we can perceive. **Perceive, believe, achieve.**

Meditation on the root chakra can release stress and increase concentration. With less stress and more concentration you can begin to get your life organized. Structure and organization are qualities of earth energy and the root chakra. Through developing courage and inner strength it is possible to start taking risks and moving forward in your chosen direction. Paralysis softens as energy flows freely though the root chakra. The job you have always wanted is now in your reach. The home you dreamed of, you are moving into. The creative project you have always wanted time to do is almost complete. Negativity is evicted and has no home where positive energy reigns. When root chakra energy is put behind a positive vision, the universe will support you in achieving your goals.

Body image is another psychological aspect of the root chakra. You may feel uncomfortable with or really dislike your body: it might be a bit of cellulite that is upsetting you or a larger issue that may have arisen after sexual or physical abuse. How you feel about your body relates to the root chakra. In some religious traditions the body is viewed as inferior to mind and spirit. Yet without a body we could not experience the mind or spirit. Body, mind and spirit work together. It is our responsibility to help them work together harmoniously. We must learn to have love and respect for our sacred body temples and protect them from ill health.

The root chakra is about our sense of stability and security. It is the natural instinct we have to find company, food, shelter, warmth and security. This translates into love, sustenance, home, work and money. When we have these basics we feel safe and secure. When

73

we don't have them we reach for false attachments that we think will make us feel safe or numb us so that we no longer care.

Addictive behaviour can arise from root chakra imbalances. Addictions ranging from cigarettes and alcohol through to drugs, sex and gambling show that the difficulties life presents can create strong desires to escape reality. These are all attachments to false pleasures. They show a lack of self-love and low self-discipline. The connection to earth through the root chakra and the energy it should supply is weakened when addictions are present. We try to feel stronger by using escape mechanisms. As energy is restored in the root chakra, life becomes worth living again and energy is free to flow upward into the other chakras bringing the many spiritual blessings they each bestow. A distorted relationship with food is another root chakra-related issue. Consider for a moment what happens when you overeat. You feel heavy and weighed down. You don't want to move. This is what happens when we have too much earth energy. We get lethargic and unable to act. An eating disorder may compensate for a lack of earth energy by actually overloading the system.

Root - Spirit

Spiritually root chakra energy is often misunderstood. The first three chakras are personal energy centres. They are responsible for us reaching our full potential as human beings. The root chakra is about our connection to earth, it is about stability and security in a physical and material sense. The sacral chakra is about our sense of self and our confidence. It is the centre that fuels the desire to be sexual and procreate. The third centre, the solar plexus is about personal power and how we assert ourselves in the world. Together, the three personal chakras provide a secure foundation from which we can know ourselves and learn to relate with others and then move out into the world feeling powerful. It is when we feel fulfilled personally that we can turn to spiritual concerns and accept the energy of the four higher chakras.

Although the root chakra is a personal centre, this does not mean it lacks spiritual qualities. This is also true of the other personal chakras; they all have a spiritual function. The spiritual function of the root chakra is grounding. When energy flows freely through the root chakra we will feel grounded. When we are grounded it is easy to move in any direction. We are able to assess a situation and move with ease. We recognize the gifts we brought into the world and are not afraid to use them. When the root chakra is balanced like a tree we are able to draw energy up from the earth and feel a strong sense of stability and inner peace. Being still and listening to root chakra energy teaches us the soul purpose of this incarnation. We come to know why we are here and begin to walk in harmony with the will of the Creator.

When we are grounded we know that:

- *we have a leg to stand on,*
- *we can put our back into it,*
- *we can stand on our own two feet,*
- *we are willing to stand up for what we believe in,*
- *we are not afraid to stand up to people.*

These popular sayings express balanced root chakra energy. We all know people who walk their talk. People who are down to earth and not afraid to get things down. These people demonstrate a strong root chakra.

WAY of

Root – Ailments

Chakras are always open and energy is always flowing through them; this way we stay alive. We need not think that our chakras are closed. What should concern us is how much energy is flowing through them and how clear is that energy. When the flow of energy through the root chakra is distorted problems can arise. Ailments can occur on any level of the body, mind or spirit. Physical problems seem to be caused by distortions in the energy field. If we work consistently with meditation, positive thinking, diet and exercise we can prevent problems occurring in the subtle energy field. By so doing we prevent physical problems.

There are a number of problems that relate to the root chakra.

Constipation – holding on, this can be on the physical level or emotional level. We often hold ourselves back, not allowing our own progress, and this is a form of constipation. Physically, we need to drink plenty of water to let go of all the waste we have been holding. Emotionally, water can be the tears that flow as we release past hurts that are holding us back.

Depression – feeling down. When energy is low the body literally becomes depressed. The shoulders drop, the breathing becomes shallow, the head drops, the digestive system packs up and life doesn't feel worth living. We can begin to uplift ourselves by changing our posture. Try opening across your shoulders, allowing your breath to deepen. Lift the front of your body, hold your head up and start to physically look forward. You will be amazed by how different you will feel. Things will change. We cannot stay depressed in an uplifted body. Hatha yoga is an excellent tonic for depression.

Lower back pain is a common problem relating to the root chakra. The best person to see is an osteopath. S/he will correct your alignment and relieve any pain. Then it is up to you to re-assess your lifestyle. What actually causes your pain? Hatha yoga is very good, especially the standing postures. Hatha yoga increases the flow of energy through the root chakra. It will also improve your posture and body awareness.

Overworking, tiredness and stress affect the root chakra, which corresponds with the adrenal glands. The adrenals are responsible for initiating the flight or fight response. This is the instinctive mechanism we use to overcome real, stressful situations, like fighting a bear. Today we are in no real danger yet we constantly activate the flight or fight mechanism through overwork. This adds stress to our bodies.

Ways of Rebalancing the Root Chakra

Root chakra ailments are quite common and many of us will have suffered one or two of them at some point in our lives. Below I introduce two simple techniques to help restore balance to the root chakra.

Grounding Exercise

This is a short exercise that can be done anywhere, but it is preferable to take a few quiet moments alone in your sacred space. This is very good for calming the nervous system, focusing the mind and getting a sense of your feet firmly connected to the ground.

Stand with your feet hip width apart, toes slightly turned in and heels out, the outside edges of your feet parallel. Have your knees very slightly bent and your spine upright. Open across your shoulders, relax your arms and begin to expand your chest as you breathe. Close your eyes gently and take three nice, deep breaths. Allow your stomach to rise on the in-breath and relax on the out-breath ... feel your whole body relaxing.

Now take your attention to your feet. Feel your connection to our mother the earth. Spread your feet and allow them to feel the movement of your breath. Breathe in through your nose and out through your feet, seven times. With each out-breath feel your feet firmly connected to the earth, imagine you are growing roots that reach down into the earth. These roots connect you to our mother the earth. They nourish and feed you. Begin to slowly draw energy up through your roots, feel the energy as it flows through your feet, your ankles, your knees, pelvis and into your belly. The energy continues to flow up your spine filling your whole body, energizing your whole body, revitalizing your entire system. Hold your posture for a few moments and be aware of all the sensations you feel as your energy flows. Feel your body grounded on mother earth.

When you are ready take a deep breath and open your eyes.

You have completed the grounding exercise.

Root Chakra Meditation

This meditation will develop your connection to the earth and help you create a greater sense of grounding.

Prepare your sacred space by cleansing the room and burning

incense or essential oils. Have cushions or a chair ready, so you can sit comfortably with your back upright, supported if necessary. When the space is ready to use, burn a red candle. Sit in front of the candle staring for a moment into the bright shining flame. Candles are symbolic of the physical body, which is represented by the wick, the flame is the energy body and the light emanating from the candle is the universal life force. As you stare into the light feel the universal life force all around you, feel the light embrace you ... Go into the light ... know that you are universal light.

- *Now close your eyes and allow your breath to deepen. Slow, even, breaths. Let your breath flow to all parts of your body. Feel the movement of breath as it relaxes every individual cell.*

- *Bring your attention to all the sensations experienced in your body. Be aware of your temperature, your weight, and your connection to the floor. Feel your base on the earth – your feet, legs, buttocks and genitals, sitting on the lap of mother earth. She is holding you. Always there giving you her love and support.*

- *Visualize the dark mysterious earth beneath the floor, under the concrete and deep below the foundations of the building. Visualize your self growing roots from your base that reach right down into the centre of the earth; into her warm belly, into her creative womb. From your roots draw her force, her love and her protection up into your being.*

WAY of

> *Fill your self full – fulfil yourself – with the*
> *earth's sacred energy. It is yours and you can*
> *take as much as you want.*
> - *Feel the pulse of the earth under your body.*
>   *Tune your entire being to the earth's vibration*
>   *... feel her rhythm inside you ... know that*
>   *you and the earth are one. Her wisdom is your*
>   *wisdom.*
> - *Be still and tune to the flow of earth energy*
>   *for 15 minutes or more.*

Listen, as the earth your mother shares her knowledge. She has a message especially for you. Let your body be still, your mind quiet and your spirit open to receive her blessing. The secret of the earth will be revealed to you. Give thanks for all blessings received.

Expect to receive: Physical health.

Working on your root chakra brings many benefits. It can help you build a strong foundation for your spiritual practice. You will quickly harvest the fruits of your work when you are disciplined enough to maintain a short daily practice. This discipline will easily transfer into other areas of your life and achieving your goals is something you will begin to fully enjoy. In my experience the rewards far outweigh the initial effort that is put in.

Through root chakra work you can gain a greater love and acceptance of your sacred body temple, and this leads to better health. As your relationship to your body improves you can begin to welcome the gifted person you really are. As you look closely your soul purpose will be revealed to you, and you will move forward knowing you are truly blessed.

SIX

THE SACRAL
Chakra

Characteristics of the Sacral Chakra

Name:	Sacral, Swadistana
Meaning:	Sacred home of the Self
Symbol:	Crescent moon
Location:	Sacrum/lower abdomen
Main function:	Provides a sense of Self

Spiritual Characteristics

Colour:	Orange
Element:	Water
Quality:	Centring
Deities:	**Africa:** *Yemonja, Òṣun, Nun*
	Akkadia/Sumeria: *Tiamat, Ishtar*
	India: *Rakini, Saraswsati,*
	Europe: *Mary, Demeter, Aphrodite*

Physical Characteristics

Gland:	Gonads: ovaries, testes
Nerve plexus:	Hypogastric plexus
Body parts:	Womb, genitals, kidney, bladder, muscles
Expression:	Love and trust in Self, responsibility to Self
Disturbance:	Low self-esteem
Physical ailments:	Lower back pain
	Fertility problems
	Gynaecological problems
	Fibroids
	Cystitis
	Kidney complaints
	Muscle cramps/spasms

Psychological Characteristics

Statement: 'I can'
Emotions in balance: All emotions are expressed
Emotions unbalanced: Afraid of emotion

Ways to Work

Oils: Clary sage, jasmine, rose, ylang ylang, sandalwood.
Gems: Carnelian, amber, orange calcite.

Sacral - Body

Situated about two inches below the navel is the second chakra, which is known as the sacral centre. This is the sacred home of your inner Self. This chakra resonates with the moon and feminine energy. It is the centre of divine inner beauty.

In your body this chakra governs the whole pelvic region. It is responsible for the ebb and flow of your emotions and feelings. Sensuality and sexuality are experienced from this chakra, which fuels the reproductive organs and the desire to procreate. This chakra is a moon centre with water as its dominant element. If we watch the moon in the night sky we will see she follows a 28-day cycle. The moon changes from the invisible dark moon to the new moon, which lights the sky with a shining crescent. Her cycle is completed with the rounded wholeness of the full moon. As the moon waxes and wanes her energy creates a magnetic pull on the sea. This causes waves and changing tides. Just as the moon affects the sea, so too she affects the waters that flow within us. Our moods swing and our tides change. For women this often occurs in relation to the 28-day menstrual cycle or moon cycle, as some women prefer to call it. Premenstrual tension and the emotional changes it can bring, such as tears, panic and angry outbursts relate to the sacral chakra and the water energy that flows through it.

The genitals, womb, ovaries, testes, bladder and the kidneys are water-related body parts. Each one is affected by our emotions. You know how it feels when you get a bit nervous, your belly goes a bit queasy, your bladder fills up and you go running to the toilet. When we feel emotional, we cry. Sexual stimulation affects the sexual organs and other body parts like the breasts, which are also governed by water energy. Sexual energy is one of the most powerful

energies we have. This energy inspired the 'Rites of Passage' cere-
monies found in many ancient cultures where, during adolescence,
young people were taught to balance this sacred energy. In modern
society where this is not taught sexual energy is often disrespected
and misused. Young people are often left vulnerable to abuse. We
should always remember that the pelvis and all its contents are
sacred. The bone at the back of the pelvis is called the sacrum,
directly from the word sacred. The energy that flows through the
pelvis like all energy is Divine.

E-motions are simply movements of energy that we interpret as
pleasure, pain, fear, etc. As the centre of emotion the sacral chakra
triggers the physical expression of our feelings. We all need to be
loved and cared for. We need to be held and nurtured and we also
need to share e-motions. These needs are part of our basic nature.
They are about our sensuality, not our sexuality. Touch and the pleasure it brings makes the sacral chakra sing. This is a centre of love
and inner beauty.

Sacral – Mind

'Learning to love yourself is the greatest love of all.' Stevie Wonder
penned these precious words. The sacral chakra houses the very self
you need to love. This is the centre of self-knowledge. It is from this
sacred centre that we come to know ourselves. Self-love must not be
confused with selfishness, being self-centred or being totally full of
yourself. No, it is quite different. It is about getting to know and love
the very essence of who you are. It is about connecting deeply with
the spirit that moves through you. Getting to know your self means
taking time with yourself. Time that is for you alone. After all if you
do not want to spend time with yourself, then why should any one

else wish to spend time with you? Meditation on the sacral chakra can help you connect deeply with the very essence of who you really are.

When energy flows freely through the sacral chakra, you will enjoy self-esteem and confidence. You will be able to make your own decisions without being afraid of what others might think. You will value your own opinion, and outcomes for yourself as well as for others, will be taken into consideration. The sacral chakra is a feminine centre. It is the place of the lover and the mother. Sometimes women get tied up in these roles and forget the Self. Many women position themselves last on an endless list of considerations. No other options are seen and eventually the resentment sets in, the feelings of being taken for granted, not having time for yourself, all the usual complaints. Well this is a chakra that asks *you* to take stock. It asks you to be still and look into the deep waters of your self. It says, *you matter*. You are the only one that can make a difference; if you have no respect for yourself and put yourself last, then you are actually teaching others that it is ok to disrespect you. If you feel worthless, free your sacral energy. Nurture and love your Self as much as you love the significant others in your life. Come home and be with your Self. *Stop now for one minute, close your eyes, breathe, and be still ....*

Creativity also springs from the well of the sacral chakra. For us to really be who we are means expressing our unique creativity. To create is to bring something new into being. We are all creative in our own special ways. For some of us this is expressed through the arts, for others it is about how we live our lives, the work we do, the children we raise. We can express our creativity in numerous styles. Yet some of us choose not to, we have become stuck. Working to rebalance the sacral chakra can release a flow of creativity. When we are creative our self-esteem gets a boost. 'I can', the statement of the sacral chakra, is heard ringing clearly from our mouths. We feel positive about ourselves and are actually better able to deal with people, relationships and other issues we may find challenging. It is vital that we find expression for the creative energy we hold inside. Think back to when you were a child, what did you love doing? Why did you stop? How was your creativity nurtured and is there a way that you can allow your creative passions to come alive again. Re-accessing your creativity at the sacral chakra helps you connect with your divine Self.

Sacral – Spirit

Being centred is the spiritual quality associated with the sacral chakra. To be centred means to move from a place of harmony. It is to act with grace and not from anger, pain or other emotions that dull clear vision. We each have a response-ability. This is the ability to act in harmony with ourselves, people around us and the environment we live in. We don't always have to re-act, instead we can honour the sacredness within ourselves. Recognizing the sacred within automatically begins the process of recognizing the sacred in others. When we stop for a few moments and bring our breath back into the sacral chakra we connect with our inner wisdom. This wisdom is the essence of the sacral chakra.

When energy is allowed to flow freely through the sacral chakra intuition will be stepped up. There is a knowing associated with this chakra. Mothers experience this sense with their children. They often know when they are in danger or hurting. Sometimes we pick up energy from people around us and tune into messages that have a deep meaning and seem to have come from nowhere. We meet people quite out of the blue, only to find we were destined to share some special moments. When I wrote my first book, so many synchronous things took place. I knew I was being guided through the entire process. My confidence soared, I had no doubts about what I was doing, I just knew it was right and that all would be well and it was.

The sacral chakra is a very special centre. It is a chakra I have a lot of affinity with; I really enjoy the quality of energy it radiates. Raising consciousness to this level makes us better people. We are friendlier, more in tune with the world, more open and self-assured. At the root we are concerned mainly with our own basic survival needs, while the sacral centre is about sharing with others. The orange ray that shines from the sacral centre has a warm welcoming glow. Orange is a colour that can excite or calm. A person with balanced sacral energy and lots of orange in their aura will be vivacious, caring and confident. They will have the ability to make people feel valued. Another person with strong sacral energy and a soft orange glow to their aura will be comforting to be around, someone people gravitate towards.

Although a strong spiritual energy emanates from this chakra, it is important to remember that it is primarily a personal chakra. A lot of change at this level is personal development, not spiritual development. Spiritual development takes place mostly in the three higher chakras – throat, brow and crown. That is not to underestimate the importance of the personal in our lives. We need to develop ourselves personally and spiritually. We need to have a healthy ego – not big, but healthy. We need to feel good about ourselves and also recognize what will help us grow towards wholeness. In my yoga training I was taught to take everything in, chew it over, and spit out what I didn't need. In this day and age with so much under the banner of 'new age' and spirituality, much of it unpalatable, it is vital to learn to recognize what will really help you evolve and grow as a person. A healthy sense of self allows for greater spiritual expansion. When the lower chakras are balanced, energy can flow freely into the higher centres and initiate powerful spiritual growth. We are growing at all times, the creator is constantly moving us towards our full potential as divine human beings.

Sacral – Ailments

Psychologically, when sacral energy flows we feel good about ourselves and can maintain a positive self-image. We are ready to get to know ourselves and accept the changes life brings. We can start creating a healthy relationship with our inner Self. Spiritually we are open to growth and development. Physically, balanced energy in the sacral chakra brings health to the pelvis and the organs held within it. When energy is distorted in any way, what we call women's problems or men's problems can occur.

Kidney problems – the kidneys are associated with the sacral chakra. They are responsible for balancing salt and water levels in the body. The kidneys can be affected by stress. Many of us do not drink enough water, and this puts additional pressure on the kidneys. To flush and cleanse your kidneys, drink water until your urine comes through clear, with no colour or odour.

Fibroids are benign growths of the uterine muscle. They occur in a high percentage of women. Although they often have no symptoms they can cause anaemia and tiredness. Visualizing the orange ray can increase the flow of energy and blood supply to this area. Imagine the colour orange washing through the sacral area, clearing any static energy and negative emotions. It is possible to reduce the size of fibroids through diet and complementary medicine.

89

Sexual abuse – when a person has been sexually abused energy closes down in the sacral chakra. Hurt, shame, betrayal and anger set up residence in this centre. These emotions mask the real beauty of the Self. It takes a lot of courage to really look beyond the pain and the tears into the deep waters of your soul and see your divine reflection. It can be done right here in the sacral chakra, the sacred home of I. Negative emotions can be evicted and love, harmony and joy can once again be allowed to flow through this precious sacral chakra. Your inner sense can be reclaimed.

Low self-esteem is a problem associated with the sacral chakra. Not feeling good enough or able enough affects a lot of people. Feeling anxious and afraid of what other people think of you can be paralysing. These problems often cause panic attacks and leave people afraid of going out and socializing. Working to develop the sacral chakra can create profound changes in how you feel about yourself. As you connect deeply to this centre you will resonate with the beauty and wisdom that resides at the very core of who you truly are.

Ways of Rebalancing the Sacral Chakra

The colour orange helps to re-vitalize and balance the sacral chakra. There are also gems and essential oils that can be used, see 'ways to work' at the beginning of this chapter. Here are two simple techniques that can help you connect with your divine inner Self.

Centring Exercise

Prepare your sacred space and take a few moments to be with your self. This exercise is good for calming the nervous system and focusing the mind. It will connect you with your inner Self and allow you to move forward feeling centred.

This practice can be done kneeling or standing. For the kneeling position, sit on your heels with spine erect. Rest your palms on your knees. For the standing position, feet are hip distance apart, body is upright, hips and shoulders are open, creating space across the chest and pelvis. Arms are relaxed at your side.

Once you are positioned take a deep breath. Let go of any tightness in your body and focus your mind on the rhythm of your breath. Then bring your attention to your sacral chakra, two inches below your navel. This is the centre of your body.

Starting at the sacral centre begin to visualize energy moving up through your belly, your chest, around your shoulders and along your arms to your hands. Feel the sensation in your hands.

Maintaining the focus and sensation of energy, inhale and begin to very slowly raise your arms up in front of you. Let your arms relax, almost as if they are moving themselves. Lift them above your head and turn the palms up to the heavens. As you exhale, slowly lower your arms back down in front of you until your palms are either resting on your knees again or falling to your side.

Repeat three to seven times. Pay attention to the breath, open your body and feel the movement of energy inside. Imagine you are on a mountaintop. The air around you is fresh and full of life-giving energy. Take that energy into your centre and let it radiate through every part of your being.

This simple exercise brings you in touch with the power of your own centre. It is extremely useful in stressful situations. It is calming, balancing and centring.

Sacral Chakra Meditation

This water meditation guides you to the sacred centre of your Self, where the holy waters flow deep within.

Prepare and cleanse your meditation space. Burn incense or essential oils for the sacral chakra. Make sure you will not be disturbed. You are deserving of time just for you. Once you are ready, light an orange candle and sit in front of it, with your back upright. As you stare into the golden light, feel your self wrapped and held by the universal life force. Go into the light, know that you are universal light.

- *With your eyes closed allow your breath to deepen. Feel your breath as it flows through and around your entire being. Energy follows each breath. Feel the energy move and focus on the sensations created.*

- *Take your attention to the fluids as they course through your body. The blood flows from the heart to every cell carrying nourishment, the cells are cleansed and the blood returns again to the heart. Open your vessels like rivers and let the waters flow.*

- *Feel the fluidity of your body as the waters expand and contract in wave-like movements. You are 80 per cent water, your every cell contains and is surrounded by water.*

- *From your base move energy up into your sacred pelvis. Open your pelvis and let the water run deep into your sensuality, sexuality, creativity and emotions.*

- *Sense the creative power of your water energy as it streams through your entire being. As a river, feel your Self returning to the infinite vastness of your mother the ocean. Rush towards her open arms and feel her wash over you, cleansing, nourishing and healing you.*

As the sea receives you, listen, for among the sound of each crashing wave is a message. The sea holds many beautiful gifts, its most precious is knowledge. As the waters flow through your being, let your spirit open to receive this great blessing. The secret of water will be revealed to you. Give thanks for all gifts received.

Expect to receive: A heightened sense of your divinity and beauty; Knowledge of your Self.

Many benefits can be gained from working on your sacral chakra. This is the centre of inner wisdom and self-knowledge. From this chakra you can begin to know, love and respect yourself. In so doing you will develop empathy and love for others. We each have a divine light that shines within. Sacral chakra work allows that divine light to shine out for the whole world to see.

Remember this is a personal chakra and the work done develops you personally and prepares you to move on to the higher chakras. It is through the higher centres that you will fulfil the spiritual work that is your destiny.

SEVEN

THE SOLAR PLEXUS
Chakra

Characteristics of the Solar Plexus Chakra

Name:	*Solar plexus, Manipura*
Meaning:	*Inner sun*
Symbol:	*Inverted triangle*
Location:	*Base of the sternum*
Main function:	*Supplies energy in the form of heat, power and enthusiasm*

Spiritual Characteristics

Colour:	*Yellow*
Element:	*Fire*
Quality:	*Feeling and Inner power*
Deities:	***Africa:*** *Ra, Hathor, Shango, Oya*
	India: *Surya, Agni, Rudra, Kali*
	Europe: *Brigit*

Physical Characteristics

Gland:	Pancreas
Nerve plexus:	Coeliac plexus
Body parts:	All digestive organs. stomach, small intestine, liver, gallbladder, spleen
Expression:	Full of energy and vitality
Disturbance:	Hypoactive/hyperactive
Physical ailments:	Digestive problems
	Food allergies
	Diabetes
	Gallstones
	Ulcers
	Liver complaints
	Hepatitis

Psychological Characteristics

Statement: I feel

Emotions in balance: Feel and express emotion easily, Joy, Happiness, Passion, Rage, Anger, Sadness

Emotions unbalanced: Controlled by emotions, Uncaring, Quick tempered, Flaring up, Violence, Despairing

Ways to Work

Oils: Rosemary, juniper, geranium, peppermint, black pepper, ginger

Gems: Citrine, tiger eye, topaz

Solar Plexus – Body

The solar plexus is found just below the sternum/breast bone. It is the radiant sun within your body. When you lift your chest and spread your arms open to stretch your body in the mornings, you are releasing energy from the solar plexus. The solar plexus supplies the body with fuel. This natural movement provides the body with a surge of energy that actually helps you wake up.

Just as the sun provides the earth with power so the solar plexus provides the body with power. The solar plexus generates energy; it is the body's powerhouse. The sun gives us light and heat, and fuels growth. Without the sun there would be no life on earth. The inner sun is also essential to life; it provides us with warmth, enthusiasm, passion and inner power. The solar plexus animates the body and keeps it alive.

Anatomically you will not find the solar plexus, but you will find the coeliac plexus, which is a group of nerves corresponding to this chakra. Digestion is a main function of the solar plexus. The fiery hydrochloric acid transforms food for life. All the digestive organs are governed by fire energy, which is the element that resonates from this centre. Fire is a powerful element that is often misunderstood. It is both friend and foe. It can create or destroy, protect or ruin. Hydrochloric acid, for example, is necessary for the digestion of food, but if it gets into the oesophagus it can cause painful heartburn and indigestion.

The liver is the largest organ in the body and is also governed by the solar plexus. The liver filters toxins from the body and stores nutrients. It is an organ that often gets overworked as a result of bad diets, pollution and drug and alcohol abuse. The liver also holds negative emotions that have not been fully digested through the digestive organs, which absorb not only nutrients, but also our experiences of life.

Solar Plexus – Mind

Psychologically, the solar plexus is responsible for digesting emotions. The experiences we encounter as we journey through life need to be swallowed, digested and absorbed. Any waste needs to be eliminated. We often choke on things, or someone makes us feel sick, or we can't stomach something traumatic that has happened to us. These experiences get held in the digestive organs and soft tissues of the body where they can cause illness. We literally hold onto old emotions for a lifetime. These old stagnant emotions can create inner conflict. The solar plexus is known as the seat of opposites because of the confusion that can be unleashed when we fail to digest the experiences life churns out to us. Anger usually hides pain, which in turn hides the treasures of your inner power. We each need time to fully digest our emotions and cleanse our systems of negativity. Stagnant emotions often hold captive an abundance of powerful energy that we must release in order to reach our full potential.

The solar plexus is the force behind our will. The will is our ability to act consciously, to make decisions and then follow them through knowing that we will achieve success. This is the powerful solar plexus energy. *Focus for a moment on a time in your life when you have felt really powerful. You have had a clear vision and then gone for it, you knew nothing could stop you from achieving your goal.* This is the solar plexus energy in action. It is dominated by fire energy, which has great clarity and direction. Balanced fire energy moves us

99

forward with enthusiasm, commitment and assertion. When we connect to the inner power of the solar plexus things always get done swiftly.

Vision and clarity are important aspects of the solar plexus. They are needed to guide our direction in life. Fire energy is directed through the eyes. If someone is happy with you or angry with you it can be seen through the expression in their eyes. A person need not say a single word, their eyes say everything. Fire energy in the eyes can reveal all: bright eyes, sad eyes, dagger eyes, truthful eyes. The eyes are said to be the windows of the soul.

Solar Plexus – Spirit

Spiritually, the solar plexus holds an abundance of wealth. Manipura, the Sanskrit name, means 'city of gems'. This is a rich chakra when we learn how to really tap into its energy. Initially it is easy to see the masculine solar plexus chakra as a place of anger, rage and destructive fire energy. But when we examine this centre further and tune to its radiant vibration we find warmth, passion and joy. This centre fuels fun and laughter. It can bring lightness to a seemingly heavy situation. Although it has a destructive quality, we must realize that destruction and death are important aspects of the wheel of life, because they create the opportunity for change and rebirth.

Rapid transformation is a function of this chakra. The destruction of war, the pain of cancer, which is war within the body, the shock of an accident, great achievements and the passion of falling in love can all profoundly affect energy at this level. These circumstances appear very different, yet they are all wake-up calls that ask us to reassess our lives. They create rapid transformation that has the potential to make us spiritually richer. Yes, we may be poorer in body and mind, yet the spirit can find an extraordinary new strength and soar to new heights as a result of the transformation created through turmoil and trauma. We are all spiritual warriors, we have the capacity to change negative energy into golden rays of sunshine.

This chakra can present many obstacles for us to overcome. Pride and ego can cause us to abuse the power we have tapped into. We should always work to empower, not dis-empower other people. Failing to give thanks for the abundant gifts we are constantly offered sends a message to the universe that we are not prepared to fully receive our riches. If we lack vision and clarity we prevent ourselves from moving forward. We can strangle any creativity we have developed by not using solar plexus energy. Not utilizing the solar plexus is one of the ways we successfully hold ourselves back. Like all the chakras it is important to keep energy flowing freely through this centre. When energy flows freely everything is possible. When energy is balanced at this chakra we are ready to ascend towards the heavens.

Solar Plexus – Ailments

This fiery centre is the origin of much imbalance and disease. Disease often has an emotional cause. How many times have you rested your hands over your solar plexus when you feel angry or upset? And how often have you not taken the time to sort out your differences with people? Instead these problems are left until they literally make us sick. The digestive system is a place where illness often begins. We are what we eat is a very true statement. When we hold onto waste either physically or emotionally we create dis-ease.

WAY of

Digestive problems As all the digestive organs are governed by the solar plexus any disturbance in this chakra can result in diseases of the digestive system. Ailments from heartburn and ulcers right through to cancer of the stomach or liver problems relate to the solar plexus and the yellow ray. Balancing fire energy can assist healing in such cases.

Fevers I am writing this book in the autumn when many people suffer from colds, flu and high fever. Fire energy is actually used to cleanse the system. Fever can have a positive function. It heats the body killing many germs. Before the onset of magic bullets (pills), fever was seen as the body's natural way of cleansing and healing itself.

Skin rashes are also the body's way of ridding itself of toxins and bacteria. Fire energy propels toxins away from the vital organs and into the skin where they do the least damage. Rashes often signal the body's need to cleanse and detox.

Exhaustion This chakra is responsible for generating energy and fuelling the entire body. It is therefore susceptible to excessive work and energy drain. It is vital that we know how to refuel and recharge our bodies through rest, diet, exercise and positive thinking. If we fail and continue to let energy flow out then we will create exhaustion and burn out, which can take a long time to recover from. There must be a balance between the amount of energy we put out and the amount of energy we draw in.

Ways of Rebalancing the Solar Plexus Chakra

Yellow, the colour of the sun is associated with this chakra. The yellow ray can be used to re-energize and balance this centre. There are of course various essential oils and herbs that have a positive effect on the digestive system. See 'ways to work'. Gems can be held during your meditation or worn on your body to help return harmony to this chakra. Below I offer two exercises that can be used to raise solar plexus energy.

Count your Blessings

For this exercise you will need a journal or several sheets of paper and some coloured pens. May I suggest you treat yourself to a nice hardback A4 book with plain paper that can be used as a *Gratitude Journal*. Put the date at the front of your journal and on the first pages give thanks for all the blessings you have received in your life so far.

If you find this difficult, think about all the time and energy you can easily waste complaining about your life and reinforcing everything that is wrong with it. Duke Ellington once said, *'I merely took the energy it takes to pout and wrote some blues.'* There is always enough time to transform negative energy into positive life enhancing energy and affirm the good things that fill your life. All you have to do is use your time positively.

Start by writing the words: *'I am truly blessed with ...'* and fill in the blanks. Let the words flow uninterrupted from the depths of your soul. When the words dry up start again, write: *'I am truly blessed with ...'*

We are all truly blessed and have so much to give thanks for. Whether it is our health, the sun that shines over us and the birds that sing. Are you grateful for the breath that you take, the children you treasure, your home that you love and your financial riches? Then make it known. We can give thanks for the goals we have achieved, our creativity, our work, the changes we are making in our lives that are helping us be more loving people. Give thanks for the challenges you face that are allowing your soul to unfold in this very moment. Whatever it is, you know that you are ever blessed.

Preferably at the eve of each day, or weekly, take time with yourself to reflect on the riches of your life and give thanks to the Creator for the blessings you have gladly received. If you really don't like routine, write in your gratitude journal whenever you feel like doing so. Of course, counting your blessings is more powerful if you do it daily. It is when we recognize and give thanks for all our blessings that we realize just how abundant and blessed we really are.

Solar Plexus Chakra Meditation

This fire meditation connects you with your inner power, and lifts your spirit high.

Prepare your sacred space. You can cleanse by fire, using a smudge stick. Burn the appropriate incense or essential oils for the solar plexus. Sit comfortably, with your back straight, in front of a yellow candle. Stare into the candle, remembering that the wick represents the physical body, the flame symbolizes the energy body and the golden light that radiates out is the universal life force. Stare into the light and allow your self to be held in its embrace. Go into the light, know that you are universal light.

- *With your eyes closed retain in your mind's eye the image of the golden flame. See the light gently flicker as you breathe in and out, in and out. Feel warmth radiating out through your entire body ... Let every cell receive golden, vibrant energy.*

- *Now take your attention to your solar plexus. This is the home of fire in your body. Visualize first the golden flame ... then the bright shining sun and eventually a beautiful roaring fire. The fire is lifting you, raising you higher and higher.*

- *As the fire burns, feel its tremendous heat. Feel its great power. This power can burn through all obstacles. Whatever stands in your path can be removed. Bring to mind anything that needs to be changed in your life ... Let the fire pass through it, see it consumed in flames. Fire consumes matter and transforms energy. Energy cannot be destroyed, it merely undergoes change.*

- *All is destroyed now except energy. You can harness the remaining energy to create whatever you need right now in your life. See what is emerging in the light of the fire ...*

- *Give energy and power to your vision. Let it grow in your mind's eye. See before your eyes your dream come true. You have the power to create anything in your life that will bring you an abundance of peace and happiness.*

Let the light shine out illuminating your vision. Let the image become crystal clear to you. Be still and see before you a message from above. Let your body be still, your mind quiet and your spirit open to receive the gift of fire. The secret of fire will be revealed to you. Give thanks and praise.

Expect to receive: Clarity and purpose in your life; Enthusiasm and confidence; The energy to move forward in your life.

You will feel totally transformed and empowered as you come to know the solar plexus chakra and begin to balance its energies. Physically you will feel stronger, less tired and full of energy. Psychologically, personal power can increase. This may show itself in improved enthusiasm for projects and more determination to put your will behind things and make them happen. Spiritually, obstacles will no longer stand in your way as you allow the divine inner fire to soar and move you forward.

This is the last of the personal chakras and many lessons can be learnt here. From this chakra we ascend to the heart chakra, which is the first of the universal chakras. This is therefore an important place of transition.

EIGHT

THE HEART
Chakra

Characteristics of the Heart Chakra

Name:	Heart, Anahata
Meaning:	Unstruck
Symbol:	Six-pointed star (interlaced triangle)
Location:	Centre of thoracic cavity behind the heart
Main function:	Transition and transformation

Spiritual Characteristics

Colour:	Green, rose pink
Element:	Air
Quality:	Compassion
Deities:	**Africa:** Maat, Oya, Erzuli
	India: Kakini shakti
	Europe: Aphrodite, Venus

Physical Characteristics

Gland: Thymus
Nerve plexus: Cardiac plexus, brachial plexus
Body parts: Heart, lungs, arms, hands
Expression: Truth (a commitment to)
Disturbance: Confusion and frustration
Physical ailments: Heart conditions
Lung problems
High blood pressure
Asthma/allergies
Fatigue
Breast cancer
Bronchial pneumonia
Immune disorders

Psychological Characteristics

Statement: I love
Emotions: As we move into the fourth chakra the emotions become more subtle. Heart chakra love asks for nothing in return. It differs from that of the sacral centre which, like the love of mother and child, holds many expectations. Emotions of the heart centre seek balance. When emotion ceases to be in balance energy falls to the solar plexus and is experienced as personal feeling.

Ways to Work

Oils: Florals: Jasmine, Rose, Neroli, Mimosa, Marigold
Gems: Rose Quartz, Green tourmaline, Emerald, Green jade, Green aventurine, Pink carnelian

WAY of

Heart – Spirit

The heart chakra is situated behind the physical heart. Remember the chakras are not little dots of energy. They are three-dimensional spheres that permeate right through your body and out into your aura.

Heart chakra energy is familiar to us all. We already realize that the heart has many qualities apart from its physical role of keeping us alive. We know the feeling of *opening our hearts* or *closing down our hearts*. We know how it feels to have a *broken heart* or to *put our heart fully into something*. Most of us know what it is to *love with all our heart* and the truth expressed when we *cross our heart and hope to die*. These energetic qualities are stimulated by the heart chakra. The heart has a very broad role.

The heart chakra sits in the middle of the seven chakras. It is symbolized by two interlaced triangles, which form a six-pointed star. This star represents the movement of energy upward from the earth and down from the heavens. It is at the heart centre that these two forces are united. This is a place of balance and divine harmony. It is at this centre that we move from the personal realms of the lower chakras into the universal consciousness of the higher chakras. It is here that we are reborn into the light. Having ascended the first three chakras and dealt with personal issues relating to survival at the root chakra, self-knowledge at the sacral chakra and personal power at the solar plexus chakra we are now ready to move from embodiment to enlightenment. Embodiment is to fully embrace the personal qualities of the lower chakras and make them part of our lives. Enlightenment is a spiritual journey, where we learn compassion and unconditional love. We learn to embrace the universal laws that govern our lives.

Compassion and unconditional love are the spiritual qualities associated with the heart chakra. These qualities are easier said than done. Real compassion is a divine gift. It requires the grace of our Creator for us really to demonstrate compassion and unconditional love. These qualities ask that we love and seek nothing in return. A lot of the time we do not realize that there are conditions attached to our love. Romantic love asks that the person loves us in return, we want to feel good, this is passion, it is the love that emanates from the third chakra. Parental love gives life and nurtures life. Although it comes closer to unconditional love and is partly unconditional, it still has expectations and is therefore love emanating from the sacral chakra. Heart chakra love is like no other. It is pure, kind and given with divine grace. It is love that passes through us from the Creator.

Heart – Mind

The heart chakra relates to air energy. Air is one of the more subtle elements, we know it exists, not so much because we see it, but because of the effect it has on things. Air creates change. Our emotions can be carried on the wings of a storm, creating chaos.

In the Yoruba tradition of West Africa, the Orisha (deities) correspond with nature's elements. Oya is the Goddess of wind. She can cause havoc in our lives through brewing up a mighty storm. She demands that old patterns and habits that no longer serve us be given to her so she can carry them away and bring forth change. Like Oya, breath holds the secret of change. When we hang on to feelings such as anger, fear and hatred, they literally stifle us. Tightening the diaphragm to induce shallow breathing is the best way to hold back emotional pain and chaos. This is something most people learn early in life. Unfortunately, continued contraction of the chest can cause physical pain, such as heart problems and immune disorders. Welcoming the Goddess Oya and breathing deeply may bring emotional storms, but it also brings the opportunity for transition. When we allow ourselves to breathe fully and open up the thoracic region, the lungs, heart and thymus are massaged and cleansed. As the diaphragm releases, the heart chakra awakens bringing love and compassion. Change is inevitable, we cannot open the heart and at the same time stay angry. The anger is transformed. This process was understood by the Ancients who both feared and loved Oya.

Moving consciousness to the heart chakra can help us have a change of heart. We can use air energy to transform the way we think. Thoughts are carried through the air; they are powerful forces that have a habit of coming true. When we think *we cannot*, we can't. When we think *we never will,* we won't. When we think *it is too late,* it is too late. When we think we are *not good enough,* we are not good enough. It is for us to change the script, rewrite the programme and make the positive changes we need in our thoughts and lives. You are the director of your own life. You are the one empowered to make changes. When you know *you can*, you will. When you know *you have all that you need within you,* you can start using it. When you know *you have an abundance of love,* you can claim it. The heart chakra is the centre of positive change and transformation. It is here that we have the opportunity to be held in the hands of harmony and float in the light of divine love.

Heart – Body

The heart chakra powers the physical heart, the lungs, respiratory diaphragm and the immune system. As long as the heart continues to beat, energy will continue to flow around your entire being. Every breath you take draws prana, the life force, into your body, animating every single cell and maintaining your life. Prana is the carrier of drug-free ecstasy. When we learn to purify and raise the quality of prana that we take into our bodies we can experience the natural high that is our birthright.

Some people can live on prana alone. Yes, it is possible. For thousands of years yogis and sages have known the secret of eternal life. You may not want to live on prana. I personally enjoy the occasional meal. But it is good to improve the quality of prana that moves within your body, through purification of the nadis, meditation and positive thinking. The foods we eat, the company we keep and the thoughts that we harbour all affect the quality of prana we take in, which in turn creates health or dis-ease in the body.

Touch is a quality associated with the heart chakra. Think about it, the impulse to touch arises from the heart, is propelled along the arms and into the hands. We touch with the hands but we reach out from the heart and we receive from the heart. When energy is blocked in the heart chakra the balance between giving and receiving can become distorted. Some people find it easy to give and hard to receive, for other people it is the opposite. We all need balance, we need to both give and receive love. This is the natural order of things, energy flows out from the heart and then returns to the heart.

Unconditional love of the heart chakra is driven to touch all people on a deep level. When we open to spirit at the heart chakra we recognize the divine in all people, and we treat them with love and respect. We do not need to sit in judgement of people's behaviour, the creator can take care of that and instead we can see the divine spirit that moves within them and encourage them to do the same. As we open to spirit we will experience a desire to see divine will reign in the world in which we live. This desire causes us to acknowledge our own soul purpose and make the necessary changes we need in our own lives to change the world. Yes! To change the world we need to start by changing ourselves, the changes we make will affect those around us, and so on, until the vibrations are felt throughout the universe.

Heart – Ailments

Loneliness is probably the most common ailment of the heart chakra. The feeling of being alone in a world where no-one can really understand you affects all of us at some time. We may be grieving over the loss of a loved one or nursing a broken heart. Loneliness often leads to isolation, we fear people will not want us around while we are low. If you are feeling lonely, empower yourself by transforming your loneliness in *alone time*. Create a healing space for yourself, meditate, write in your journal, enjoy bathing in the essential oils of the heart chakra, show love and compassion to yourself.

Immune problems We are seeing an increase in immune system-related disorders. Maybe it is, as some people think, because life in the modern world is divorced from natural laws? Are illnesses such as HIV, cancer and ME caused by spiritual crisis? Do they beg us to reassess life, love ourselves more and honour the spirit that moves through us? Immune-related disorders can use the green ray of the heart chakra to assist the healing process. Green is the colour of new growth, its vibration is used to calm and repair damaged tissue.

114   **Heart attack** Swami Vishnudevananda said, *'The heart never* *attacked anybody. We attack the heart.'* We constantly abuse the heart through holding onto negative emotions, employing shallow breathing, eating foods that are poisoning us, and working in jobs that are seriously damaging our health. To prevent heart problems, open the heart chakra and listen to the changes you need to make in your life. We all know what is good for us, we just refuse to listen sometimes.

Pain Life has a habit of dealing us trauma after trauma, starting from a very early age. Many of us are holding a lifetime's pain in our hearts yet we refuse to acknowledge that we are hurting. Instead we are just angry inside and lack faith in the universe. Our hearts are literally dying to breathe again, to open up and let our love show. When we face the pain that we hold in our hearts we can release it and let our inner light shine out. Know that underneath your pain lies a desire to love and be loved.

Ways of Rebalancing the Heart Chakra

The most powerful exercise for tuning to the universal chakras is meditation. The energies at this level are subtle and therefore subtle techniques are required. Keep working on the lower chakras, with your grounding and centring exercises. Continue to count your blessings using your gratitude journal and spend more time in meditation.

Heart Chakra Meditation

Your journey so far has transported you up through the lower personal chakras. You have now reached the heart centre, home of transition. From here you will move into the universal chakras. The

115

WAY of

air meditation that follows connects you to your boundless source of love and compassion.

Prepare your sacred space by cleansing the environment. Burn sweet-smelling floral incense or essential oils. Put flowers in the room and light a rose pink or green candle. When you are ready, sit in a meditative pose, in front of the candle. Gaze at the candle's light. See the aura of the candle and feel the light of your own aura enveloping your body. See the candle's gentle pulse and feel the pulse of your own energy field. Become one with the light. Know that you are universal light.

- *As you sit in your meditative posture, gently close your eyes and focus on the movement of your breath. Feel your chest expand and contract. Be aware of the air as it enters your nostrils ... throat ... chest ... and abdomen; feel the air then leave the abdomen ... chest ... throat ... and nostrils. Follow this rhythm five times.*

- *Open your heart to love. Relax your body, let your mind be still and allow your spirit to soar, rising high. Fully open your chest and heart chakra. Allow the winds of change to blow through your entire being. The wind will purify your being, cleanse you, release you from all limitations.*

- *You are free, free as a bird flying high above the clouds. Your body is light and full of love. Love is within you, it permeates your every cell.*

Love is all around you, caressing you. From deep within your heart let your love flow. Touch your family and friends with your love. Touch your neighbours, your local community, your society, the world. Let your love flow out and touch all people everywhere. All living beings.

- *The love you give out multiplies and returns to you. So let your heart open wide to receive all the love and compassion, that as a child of the universe, is justly yours.*

- *Feel the vibration of love and compassion in your soul, hold the sensation, be there now experiencing love and radiating love in all directions.*

As the spirit of air moves through you, touching you with love, feel her deep in your soul for she carries a message. Let your body be still, your mind quiet and your spirit open to receive. The secret of air will be revealed to you. Receive your blessings and give thanks.

Expect nothing: Give unconditionally, believe that the universe will always provide for you.

Transformation takes place from the inside out, it is not something that is applied to the surface. Working on the heart chakra requires patience, discipline and a genuine desire for spiritual growth. Take your time working on the heart chakra. Remember that as one of the universal centres the benefits you will receive will be subtle but great. Spiritual development resonates at the very core of your being and from here it creates profound change.

117

NINE

THE THROAT
Chakra

Characteristics of the Throat Chakra

Name:	*Throat, Vishuddha*
Meaning:	*Purification*
Symbol:	*Circle*
Location:	*Throat C3 – C5*
Main function:	*Communication*

Spiritual Characteristics

Colour:	*Blue*
Element:	*Ether*
Quality:	*Vibration, sound, voice*
Deities:	**Africa:** *Tehuti, rúnmìlà, òrúnmìlà*
	India: *Sadasiva, Saraswati*
	Europe: *Hermes, Mercury*

Physical Characteristics

Gland:	*Thyroid*
Nerve plexus:	*Pharyngeal plexus, cervical plexus*
Body parts:	*Throat, ears, mouth*
Expression:	*'Open to Spirit' awareness of and communication with spirit*
Disturbance:	*Limited awareness*
Physical ailments:	*Sore throats*
	Loss of voice
	Thyroid problems
	Mouth ulcers
	Teeth and gum conditions
	Headaches
	Ear infections

Psychological Characteristics

Statement: *I speak, I hear*
Emotions in balance: *Stillness, peacefulness and harmony*
Emotions unbalanced: *Restless, anxious*

Ways to Work

Oils: *Frankincense, camomile, sandalwood*
Gems: *Blue lace Agate, Lapis lazuli, Blue quartz, Turquoise, Lazulite*

Throat – Spirit

The throat chakra is a powerful spiritual centre that resonates at a high frequency. As the name suggests, it is positioned in the throat region, between the third and fifth cervical vertebrae.

The primary function of this chakra is communication. Firstly, it is about communicating with your creator. It also connects you to your inner Self and the **G**ift **O**f **D**ivinity (**GOD**) that lies within. This chakra holds answers to many spiritual questions. Through the throat centre you can learn to accept your true nature and acknowledge your divinity. This chakra connects deeply with your soul and allows you to listen as your soul speaks. It is also about communication with others through words and creativity. Psychic ability and communion with those from other realms resonates at the throat centre. We can learn to connect with our spirit guides, ancestors, angels and helpers through the throat chakra and the ether element.

Ether, the subtlest of the elements, is closely aligned with pure spirit. The throat chakra gives rise to ether energy in the body. Ether is the space through which the other four elements, air, fire, water and earth are created. It is a container; without it nothing could exist. This container holds information that we can tap into. We have all heard the expression *'It just came out of the blue'*. This saying is used when information is suddenly remembered or gained seemingly from nowhere. When we study spiritual laws we begin to recognize the relationship between all things. Blue is the colour associated with the throat chakra. Rather than appearing from nowhere, information literally comes out of the ether. Ether is the original cyberspace. An archive of everything that was, is and ever shall be, it is known as the akashic record, or the collective unconscious.

Telepathy is far more common than we realize. Can you remember a time when you thought about someone and they telephoned you, or even turned up on your doorstep, or you sensed something would happen and it did? We all have a sixth sense that can be developed through trusting in its existence. Opening the throat chakra and resonating fully with ether helps us log onto and communicate with the powerful energy that moves within and around us at all times.

Throat – Mind

The throat chakra is concerned with creation and bringing things into being through sound. From the ancients we learn that the entire universe was created from pure vibrational sound. Our thoughts have a vibration, as do our words. They each hold energy that is capable of manifesting what we are thinking or saying. Therefore it is vital at this level to develop a heightened awareness of energy, its vibration and how we use it. When the mind holds positive thoughts and images, life will be positive. When we learn to really identify happiness, beauty and real wealth, we will see that our lives are already overflowing. You cannot buy happiness because you already own it. It is your choice to express it whenever you wish. You are rich in the love of your creator, who gave you everything you need and then left you to find it. Many of us are still looking because we choose to look outside of ourselves for happiness instead of within. We claim negativity and hold onto it tight. We choose to believe in failure over success and wonder why we fail. When we think we are depressed, depression soon follows. Remember, you are writing the script. The universe is supporting your thoughts. *Think for a moment about some of your achievements and remember how much positive energy you generated at those times in your life.* When you are

123

WAY of

positive and put all your energy into something, you know you can create success. A clear flow of energy through the throat chakra will help you achieve your soul purpose.

Vishuddha, the Sanskrit name of this chakra, means purification. As we ascend the chakras, moving into the higher spiritual realms, it is important to cleanse the nadis (energy pathways). We can cleanse through, fasting, pranayama and positive thinking. If toxic energy exists at this level it lowers the vibration, clouds communication and limits spiritual experience. When energy is clear this powerful chakra can be utilized in many ways. Dreams, meditation and divination bring prophecies that help us on our spiritual journey. Our thoughts are free to move through past, present and future bringing understanding. We can create a harmonious life filled with the wisdom and knowledge of our creator and the love and beauty of our mother the earth.

Throat – Body

Physically, the throat chakra corresponds to sound and hearing. Music is a powerful healer. Sound vibrations can resonate through the entire body creating harmony. Kind words are capable of lifting the spirit. The ancients used mantras, which are repetitions of sacred sounds. These words clear the mind in preparation for meditation.

> *Try repeating the mantra 'Aum' for five minutes. It will calm the nervous system and bring relaxation to your body and mind. Prolong each sound Aaaa-uuuu-mmmm, Aaaa-uuuu-mmmm, Aaaa-uuuu-mmmm, Aaaa-uuuu-mmmm, Aaaa-uuuu-mmmm, Aum.*

When the mind is clear your system is open to receive universal energy. At the throat chakra this energy may manifest in the form of visionary art, which can be very healing. Creativity is a characteristic of the throat chakra, but it has a particular quality. At the sacral chakra we are concerned with art that is an expression of self. At this level art arises with little effort. Colours can emerge as paintings on canvas, music rings in your ears and is captured by your voice or another instrument. Poems appear as if they wrote themselves. Have you ever had the experience where for a moment all is well in your world, you feel high and allow your self to be and to create? It is as if a powerful force just took your hand and created for you. This is visionary art that has a message for the world.

The above experience is a good example of energy flowing freely through the throat chakra, but the throat chakra is often blocked and in need of attention. Many of us have problems expressing ourselves verbally and saying what we are really feeling. Sometimes we fail to explore our creativity, leaving a part of ourselves unfulfilled. We all need sacred space and yet how many of us really honour this need in ourselves. We do not learn early in our lives the importance of the sacred, both within our selves and in our environments. When the throat chakra is blocked the flow of energy is reduced between the chakras in the head and those in the body. Ideally, energy should be free to flow throughout all the chakras, allowing them to work together in harmony.

Throat – Ailments

Spiritual crisis and alienation from your core can cause weakness throughout your system. At this level in particular ailments tend to be more spiritual than physical. Re-addressing your spiritual needs and increasing time spent in spiritual practice can help bring harmony to this chakra and consequently your life.

Grief Emptiness and the pain of loss resonate at the throat chakra. Grief has two aspects. We feel grief for a loved one whose soul has left their physical body. This suffering can also trigger a deeper pain. Deep pain is caused because as human beings we exist within duality – the creator and the created. Deep inside we long to re-unite with our creator. We hold a subtle memory of our blissful existence before duality. We can return to a sense of oneness through intense spiritual practice.

Verbosity Talking too much wastes a lot of energy and can prevent us from simply being. Talking fills empty spaces. It changes the vibration by creating activity where there is a fear of silence. Silence is a creative energy. When we are comfortable with silence much can emerge. *Next time you are indulging in too much talking, ask yourself, 'Is there something I am afraid of right now?'*

Exhaustion is a problem that affects many people living in modern societies. Not having enough space affects the throat chakra. We fill every moment in every day from sun up to sun down, leaving too little time and space in our lives. We exist in concrete jungles divorced from nature and then wonder why we feel ill. Eventually nature catches up with us and the adrenals, liver and nervous system become totally run down. The body needs a break and takes one; we refer to it as a break-down. Your body signals you to stop! If you don't, all your body can do is take drastic measures and *break*. We wonder why we are suddenly suffering from a serious illness or have had a bad accident. Such measures have an immediate effect, they cause us to stop and focus on the important things in our lives, like our health. *Each day has 24 hours or 1,440 minutes. How much of* *that time do you take to love and nurture your body, mind and spirit?* Enjoy a much-needed break before your system does it for you.

Eating disorders Anorexia, bulimia and constant dieting are problems relating to the throat chakra. Eating disorders can disrupt the body's endocrine system, which is responsible for producing and balancing hormones. The thyroid gland situated in the throat area is responsible for metabolism – which is the rate at which we use energy in the body. The metabolic rate has a direct effect on weight. Psychological issues about how much space we take up in the world often cause obsessions with weight. It may be that carrying too much weight is a protective measure to hide a vulnerable person. A person with very low self-worth who doesn't really want to be here may become anorexic. The sacral and throat chakras are closely connected. Working on the throat and sacral chakras can help people suffering from eating disorders.

Ways of Rebalancing the Throat Chakra

Spirit Guides

Spirit guides are helpers from other realms. They can take many forms – angels, ancestors, animal totems, disincarnate beings – and occasionally they take the form of earth beings. Spirit guides are with us at all times, they walk alongside us and are available to offer assistance whenever we are ready both to ask for help and to listen to the information we are given. They do not interfere; they simply wait for us to call on them. They communicate through the throat chakra, but the sensations can be felt in any of the chakras depending on which chakras are clear and open enough to receive. For example your experience may be kinesthetic – you may feel a sensation in your body and know your guide is with you: this involves the root chakra. You may receive an emotional response which involves the sacral chakra, or maybe you just know in your belly, which is a signal from your solar plexus. At the heart level questions are easily answered as thoughts and fears give way to an overwhelming sensation of love; a love that lets you know all is well and that you are not alone. At the throat voices of wisdom are heard offering divine guidance. The third eye provides sensory perception, and dreams or images appear in answer to your questions. The crown offers total revelations; all is revealed, going far beyond the senses into a place of ultimate knowledge.

Connecting with your Spirit Guides

Your spirit guides are there to help you journey along your spiritual path. You can ask for assistance at any time. The secret, however, is to learn to hear your guides as they whisper words of wisdom. Working on all your chakras and practising meditation will help you prepare. Cleansing and purity of your nadis will affect the quality of information you receive. Opening to Spirit is like tuning a radio. Imagine you are only used to hearing interference, it is hard to believe what clarity and beauty could be heard if your radio was fine-tuned. The same is so of the energy body; it needs fine-tuning in order to receive clear uplifting transmissions. Trusting is an important starting place. When you trust that you are not alone and know that your guides are with you, they will reveal themselves to you.

Have a pen and your journal ready to record the guidance you receive. Remember clear questions attract clear answers.

- *When you are ready sit comfortably and begin tuning to the rhythm of your breath. With each inhalation go deeper into your being and with each exhalation let go of all limitations. Nothing is holding you back. You are ready to soar, ready to open to spirit.*

- *At the centre of your being visualize a golden light. Feel this light begin to vibrate and spin. Each rotation moves slowly out into your body, until your whole being is filled with this shimmering, golden light. Let the light shine and fill every cell in your body. Feel your whole being bathed in golden light.*

- *Feel the golden light move beyond your body, embracing you. You are held in this bright, shining, golden light. You feel uplifted and safe, as your being vibrates from its inner core right out into your aura. Enjoy the sensation of silence and the boundless space. Open your energy field and allow yourself to fully receive.*

- *As you breathe feel the golden light reaching out, embracing your spirit guides, calling them close to you. Feel the great surge of energy as you acknowledge their presence.*

- *Know that they are with you now ... ask for the guidance you need. There is nothing spirit guides cannot help you with, they are all powerful and all knowing, they are universal messengers here to bless you with knowledge from the most high.*

- *Feel their vibration, sense them, hear their voices, see the golden light deepen, revealing everything you need to know right now. Be still and listen carefully with all your chakras. Honour the energy that flows through your being offering you guidance.*

- *When your guidance is complete and you feel ready, return to the movement of your breath. Draw the golden light back into the centre of your being, know that it is always there for you to call on whenever you need guidance.*

- *Open your eyes. Take your pen and journal to record in words or images the message you have received.*

Throat Chakra Meditation

You have now reached the throat chakra. Communication is brought forth from the spinning of the throat chakra. Sound and hearing from all planes of existence come together in this chakra. This meditation connects you to the wisdom, of all that was, is, and ever shall be.

Arrange your sacred space. Burn frankincense to remove any negative energy. Light a sky-blue candle and sit comfortably in your chosen meditative position. Look into the light, see beyond the light, let the light expand and embrace you. Merge with the light, know that you are universal light.

As you ascend the chakras, entering meditation should become easier for you. With continued practice your breath automatically deepens and your mind begins to slow down.

- *Close your eyes and observe the changes occurring in your physical body ... in your breath ... in your nervous system ... in your consciousness ... in your energy field. Be aware of all the different sensations. Tune into the vibration of your energy.*

- *As you breathe listen for the subtle vibrational sound of your energy. Hear it on your in-breath, hear it on your out-breath. Repeat this sound silently to your self. This is your own unique healing sound. This sound directly links you to the ether element and the etheric plane. Your helpers in the etheric realm will hear your sound.*

- *Continue silently repeating your sound. You will feel a great charge of energy as your helpers surround you.*

- *When you are completely elated by this force and sure help is with you, then you can ask any question for which you require an answer ... guidance can come in any form. It may be an image, sensation or a sound. Simply remain receptive.*

Open your whole being to the ether energy. Let spirit speak to you. Let your body be still, let silence surround you as your spirit opens to receive. The secret of ether will be revealed to you. Accept the blessings of ether and sing your praises.

Expect to receive: Spiritual guidance; A reminder of your soul purpose and what is destined for you in this life.

The spiritual journey is not always easy. Working at the throat chakra requires regular practice. Purification techniques are essential to clear the nadis and cleanse the energy field. Increasing time spent in meditation, creative pursuits and silence will enhance energy at the throat chakra.

Enhanced energy at the throat chakra deepens your connection to spirit. As energy flows freely you will open to a wisdom and knowledge that has the potential to propel you towards the light of your Creator.

TEN

THE BROW

Chakra

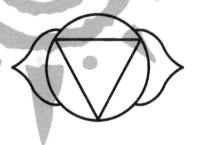

Characteristics of the Brow Chakra

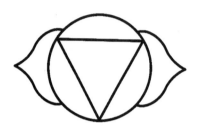

Name:	Third eye, Ajna
Meaning:	Perception
Symbol:	Two snake's heads and eagles' wings
Location:	Slightly above and between the eyebrows
Main function:	Seat of wisdom, centre of inner vision

Spiritual Characteristics

Colour:	Indigo
Element:	Dark and Light
Quality:	Vision
Deities:	*Africa:* Horus, Utcheat/Uraeus, Òsumaré
	India: Shiva/Shakti –Ardhanarishvara, Tara
	Europe: Hermes, Mercury

Prophets and great teachers:
> *Buddha, Jesus, Allah*

Physical Characteristics

Gland:	*Pineal*
Nerve plexus:	*Autonomic nervous system*
Body parts:	*Left and right cerebral hemispheres, mind function*
Expression:	*Insight and knowledge*
Disturbance:	*Dismissive of your own spiritual experience*
Physical ailments:	*Learning difficulties*
	Brain tumour
	Blindness
	Deafness
	Pain
	Dyslexia
	Insomnia

Psychological Characteristics

Statement: *I see/I know*
Emotion: *Stillness of body–mind*

Ways to Work

Oils: *Frankincense, sandalwood*
Gems: *Sapphire, lapis lazuli, sodalite, jet, black opal, azuite*

Brow – Spirit

Ajna chakra is more commonly known as the third eye. It is situated slightly above and between the eyebrows. This is a centre of divine wisdom and knowledge. It is the home of inner vision. From here we can visualize our destiny and make it our reality. Whatever you can perceive, you can achieve.

Through this chakra we can generate lasting peace. This is why advanced meditation practices concentrate on the third eye. Daily silent meditations for 30 minutes, with gentle breathing and attention focused on your third eye, can totally transform your life. It will allow you to connect deeply with your divine inner core. Ajna chakra can create balance in your life and bring knowledge of the natural laws that govern each and every one of us.

As you fully open to spirit at this chakra, through disciplined spiritual practice, you will experience an altered state of consciousness. A trance-like state that brings harmony to Nekhebet and Uatchet or ida and pingala. These are spiralling life currents with opposing qualities. Nekhebet or ida is negative or yin while Uatchet or pingala is positive or yang. Everything is made up of varying degrees of these energies. They flow like day and night and the sun and moon. Together they weave life's rich web of activity. Sometimes we are yin – inert like the night – and other times we are yang – active like the day. But our creator has also blessed us with the ability to create an energetic resting place. A place of total stillness and bliss which is known as the shushumna. When energy ceases to flow through ida and pingala, it is free to enter the shushumna, which is the neutral central column. All movement stops as energy flows towards the sacred light of the divine.

The Egyptian caduceus symbolizing the three main nadis – Ida, Pingala, Shushumna or Nekhebet, Uatchet, Tehuti

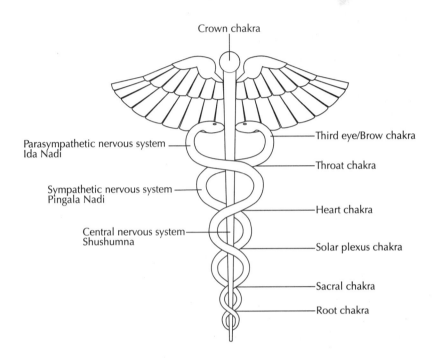

As we rest in this sacred inner place our energy is rebalanced. Our perceptions are expanded and we see beyond ordinary reality. This is a place of healing. As energy flows through the shushumna, we can clear negative karma from past, present and future. The soul knows no boundaries. We can start to manifest our soul purpose.

The ancients thought of ajna chakra as the seat of the soul. It is the gateway to knowledge and expanded consciousness. Through spiritual practice you can rise above limitations and ascend towards liberation. This is the last chakra before we unite again with our creator at the crown chakra.

Brow – Mind

Ajna chakra is one of two centres in the head. It governs the intellect – the process of thinking. Our aspirations are made manifest from here. This is the place of vision and insight. When we are able to visualize our direction in life it is easier to walk forward confidently. Positive thinking leads to mastery. You are capable of whatever you put your mind behind. If you believe in failure, failure will hold you in its grip. Likewise, success is yours if it is what you see for yourself. Inner peace and lasting happiness are available for you to claim. They are your spiritual inheritance.

The creative power of the third eye has been known throughout time in numerous cultures and spiritual traditions. It has been called the soul eye. In ancient Egypt it was known as the eye of Heru, in China the eye of Buddha, in the Caribbean Rasta far-I, and in West Africa, Ẹlẹ̀dàá. In India the third eye is known as Bindu or the black dot of all creation. The ancients tell us that we can use the power of the third eye through meditating on its location. When your mind is clear you can begin to see your destiny mapped out before you.

Without inner vision we stumble in the darkness, not quite knowing why things are always going wrong in our lives. Because this chakra balances light and dark, it can bring order out of chaos. It helps us face the darkness and find answers to our many questions. Light can only shine out of darkness. Imagine you are on the road, it is getting dark and you are unsure of your route. The first thing you will do is stop, possibly at a petrol station where you can refuel and ask for help. Armed with information you can continue your journey, travelling safely in the right direction. Losing our direction in life requires similar tactics. Stopping is the first stage. The third eye is akin to the petrol station: a place where you can refuel and get help. Meditating on the third eye shines light into the darkness and illuminates the soul. The answers you have been searching for appear clearly once you begin looking with your soul eye. When we are despairing and full of fear, it is time to stop for a moment and re-assess. Meditation on the third eye is the perfect place to begin because it brings the spiritual knowledge we really long for.

Brow – Body

Physically, the third eye corresponds to the pineal gland. Western medicine once considered this gland to be of little importance. It appears to crystallize with age, which has led mystics to believe that it has the qualities of crystal and is, in fact, our inner crystal, capable of absorbing, storing and transmitting light energy. These qualities, coupled with the visionary aspects of the third eye, help us understand the spiritual function of the pineal gland. It seems that it is already programmed with knowledge that we simply need to decode.

The third eye is a powerful psychic centre. Not only can we develop a greater awareness of our own spiritual consciousness, but some individuals develop clairvoyant skills enabling them to offer psychic readings to other people and see into other realms. Psychic powers should never be abused, they are a gift sent by the creator to test us. If used wisely they will advance us on our path towards enlightenment, if abused we may experience a rapid decline in spiritual development.

When energy flows freely through ajna chakra you will notice changes in your vibration, you will experience freedom. Ajna chakra vibrates at the level of the higher mind, the celestial realm, home of the stars. Two serpents and an eagle are depicted at this centre representing harmony between ida and pingala – the balance of opposites. Twin serpents, ida and pingala, meet at ajna chakra and from here energy is lifted up on eagle's wings. This symbolizes energy moving from the root chakra upwards through all the chakras and transcending ordinary consciousness into a realm of extra-ordinary consciousness. Wings carry us towards the stars, towards the home of our creator. Here we have the opportunity to gain knowledge. A chance to hear sacred words of wisdom. When energy is restricted at ajna chakra, spiritual awareness will be limited. The rational mind will be asked to account for everything, which of course it cannot do.

Due to the step-down process explained in chapter two (page 31), spiritual balance will also step down and create physical balance. Working on the third eye helps balance the left and right cerebral hemispheres of the brain. Science now recognizes that they operate independently, the right side having a spatial awareness and the left side a linear awareness. I will use an analogy to explain the difference of each hemisphere. Picture someone creatively juggling, enjoying the balls as they move through the air and catching them without difficulty. They make the exercise look very easy. This person is using the right side of the brain – intuitive and spatial awareness. Now ask the same person to develop a mathematical equation detailing the exact movements and speed of the balls as they fly through the air and they are likely to have a problem. It is also quite likely that the person who can create the mathematical equation cannot actually juggle, because this person excels by using the left side of the brain – logical and linear awareness. Most people tend to be dominant on one side of the brain. We are either more intuitive or more rational. Ideally, we need a balance of left and right brain activity. Working on ajna chakra helps create this balance. This was known in ancient Egyptian and Indian spiritual traditions: both had systems for stimulating ajna chakra and developing harmony between the brain's two hemispheres.

Brow – Ailments

Physical Pain Meditating on ajna chakra can help relieve physical pain. Ajna chakra resonates with the nervous system and can have a calming and regulating effect. Deep relaxation of the nervous system releases muscular contraction that traps nerves and causes pain (see relaxation and breathing in chapter 4, page 60). Thoughts, which we know are very powerful, can be used to alleviate pain. *Visualize the body part or parts that are painful. Breathe deeply into them. Imagine the pain slowly dispersing with each breath. Visualize the pain being gently lifted up and away on a cloud. As you breathe deeply into the area begin to replace the pain with the healing colour blue.* This is very effective when practised regularly. Pain can be removed or greatly reduced through using this simple visualization technique.

Migraine Headaches are characterized by severe head pain, usually to one side of the head only, which is sometimes accompanied by nausea and sore eyes. Like many of the ailments mentioned they require a medical check to rule out more serious problems. Migraines are often triggered by stress, so try to reduce stress levels as much as possible. Learning to meditate can be very helpful. Use meditation techniques for any of the chakras. Make sure plenty of water has been drunk and that the bowels are being regularly emptied. Poor elimination is a common cause of headaches. Also check that your breathing is full, to allow a good supply of oxygen to the brain. If headaches remain after the above pointers are checked use the visualization techniques mentioned above.

Mental exhaustion Like all body parts the brain and mind become tired. If we ignore all signs and refuse to slow down and rest we will become mentally exhausted. Simple tasks will become difficult. We

WAY of

will start to make silly mistakes at work or home. Confusion, anxiety and stress will soon follow, leaving us feeling hopeless and irritated. If this is a familiar pattern rest and relaxation are called for. At work, burn incense (if possible) and place crystals in your environment. Stop for five minutes each hour to stretch and release any tension in your neck that is reducing energy flow to your head. At home take long baths using relaxing essential oils.

Psychic overload This is when there is a lot of psychic interference coming either from your own system or from people and the environment around you. Ideally, we should be able to tap into psychic energy when we choose and not feel overpowered by it. We don't want to be flooded with uncontrollable insights that make us feel weakened and vulnerable. This can happen when the nadis require further cleansing and the lower chakras need rebalancing. If you feel that your chakras are too open and you are picking up a lot of negative energy take time to close down your energy field (see chapter four, page 65). Also cleanse your system and immediate environment using techniques from chapter four (pages 53–66).

Ways of Rebalancing the Brow Chakra

Deep focus and concentration are required to develop the third eye. Changes occurring at this centre are subtle in vibration and profound in effect. An expanded awareness of subtle energy is needed to sense the vibrational shifts that offer you boundless gifts.

Crystal Meditation

I suggest you use the precious gem lapis lazuli for this meditation. It was highly regarded by the Ancient Egyptians for its healing properties and balancing effect on the third eye. It offers protection and when worn is known to keep negative energy at bay and bring good fortune. Lapis works on the spiritual, emotional and physical levels to reduce pain. It also brings balance to the endocrine and nervous systems, making it a powerful crystal for many ailments. However, the main reason I am suggesting lapis is because of its capacity to heighten meditation and stimulate inner vision.

Keep your journal and pen by your side in case anything arises in your meditation that you wish to make a note of. This is your special time, so make sure you will not be disturbed.

Cleanse your lapis in salt water before use and prepare yourself for meditation.

Sit by your altar and light the candles. Breathe evenly and fully; allow your body to be upright but relaxed. You are entering a place of deep meditation, a place of stillness and inner beauty, a place of love and light.

Place the lapis lazuli in your right hand, which is your giving hand. You are offering everything you don't need to the universe. The universe gladly receives the energy and transforms it; all negative energy can be neutralized. Keep your breathing even and focus on your third eye. You are clearing your entire system, getting rid of all your negative energy, tiredness, fatigue, pain, etc. Everything you don't need – your doubts, anxiety, fears – let them go ... let them go. Empty yourself and create space for the divine to enter.

143

WAY of

Continue releasing, letting go, making space in your body temple for all the spiritual riches that await you. Be still and meditate on your third eye for around fifteen minutes.

Your system is now clear and you are ready to receive your divine blessings. Place the lapis in your left hand, which is your receiving hand. Breathe evenly and sense the energy pouring in through your left hand. Feel your vibration gently lifting. Open to spirit, open wide and allow the divine to enter.

For the next fifteen minutes simply **be**.

Know that you are completely divine, blessed with the power and love of our Creator.

Brow Chakra Meditation

Your ascension is almost complete. You have reached the stars, the celestial realms. The dark night sky is spotted with shining light. The brow chakra takes you into the darkness where all the colours of light reside. This light meditation brings illumination, vision and insight. Allow 30 minutes, 5 minutes on each centre.

This meditation is more powerful if done during Brahmahurta, which is between the dark hours of four and six in the morning. The Ancients always knew this to be true and it has now been backed by science. During these hours, levels of the hormone melatonin, which is produced by the pineal gland, are at their highest. Research states that high levels of melatonin are present during mystic experiences and psychic visions.[1]

Prepare your sacred space, rise early and burn your incense or essential oils. Light an indigo or black candle. Sit in front of your burning candle and gaze at the bright shining flame. See all the colours of light in the flame. Black, blue, green, violet, red, orange, yellow. These colours create universal light. Enter the light, feel your self lifted in light. Go into the light knowing that you are both darkness and light. You are pure vibrational energy.

- *Sit upright, close your eyes and allow your self to enter a meditative state. Breathe easily and relax your whole being.*

- *Take your attention to your root chakra and focus on the colour red ... let the red ray fill your being ...*

- *Raise your attention to the sacral chakra and focus on the colour orange ... let the vibration of the orange ray fill your being ...*

- *Raise your attention to the solar plexus chakra, focus on the colour yellow ... let the yellow ray permeate your entire being ...*

- *Lift your energy to the heart chakra, home of the colours green and rose pink ... feel the colours spreading throughout your body ...*

- *Now on to the throat chakra, focus on the colour blue ... allow the blue ray to flow into your whole being ...*

- *Ascend to the brow chakra, see all the colours of the rainbow merge before your eyes. On this black screen you will see a golden light, a shimmering, flickering*

145

*light that emerges like the sun from darkness as it
enters the celestial light. As you go into the light
sense all around you the stars, angels, Gods and
Goddesses, ready to receive you, welcoming you,
gesturing you home.*

- *Absorb the vibration and powerful energy ...
fill your being until it overflows ... hear the whispers
of wisdom. Open your spirit and receive all you can,
for you will not stay long. You will leave giving
thanks and knowing that you can return again at will.
The secret of light is revealed to you.*

Have no expectation, be open to receive the gifts offered to you from the universe.

If you have completed the brow chakra exercises you will begin to feel a change in your vibration. If you practise regularly others will soon notice the changes in you. Light will vibrate from the very core of your being. This chakra lies amid the spiritual triad made up of the throat, the brow and the crown chakras. Perhaps for us earth beings it is the most important of the three, because it provides us with spiritual insights and knowledge that guides us as we journey through the terrain we know as life. This chakra blesses you with inner vision and enables you to bring spirit down to earth.

Notes

1   *See* Where Science and Magic Meet, *by*
     Serena Roney-Dougal, Element Books, 1991.

ELEVEN

THE CROWN
Chakra

WAY of

Characteristics of the Crown Chakra

Name:	Crown, Sahasrara
Meaning:	One thousand – Infinity
Symbol:	Circle
Location:	Anterior fontanel
Main function:	Liberation

Spiritual Characteristics

Colour:	Gold, Violet
Element:	Pure Spirit
Quality:	Fulfilment
Deities:	**Africa:** Ausar (Osiris), Olódùmárè
	India: Shiva, Varuna, Aditi
	Europe: Hermes, Mercury
	All Supreme Gods

Physical Characteristics

Gland:	*Pituitary*
Nerve plexus:	*Central nervous system*
Body parts:	*Transcends the physical body and controls esoteric anatomy*
Expression:	*Satchitananda – Truth knowledge bliss*
Disturbance:	*Ignorance of one's spiritual nature*
Physical ailments:	*Depression Paralysis Multiple sclerosis*

Psychological Characteristics

Statement: *I am (divine)*

Emotions in balance: *Peak experience, Peace, Oneness*

Emotions unbalanced: *Disorientation, Constant worry, Fragmentation*

Ways to Work

Oils: *Lavender, bay laurel, valerian*

Gems: *Amethyst, diamond, selenite, clear quartz, pearl*

*Sahasrara chakra is the still quiet place of
oneness. The realm of anandamayakosha –
bliss sheath. This is the destiny of all spiritual
practice. It is our birthright to know and dwell,
at our will, in a state of peaceful bliss.*

Opening to Spirit, *page 262*

Crown – Spirit

The crown chakra lies at the top of the head. It is positioned over the place we call the *soft spot* on a newborn baby's head. This is thought to be where the soul enters the physical body at birth and departs at the time of death. The soul enters and takes up residence in the third ventricle of the brain. The third ventricle is said to be the actual seat of the soul.

The crown chakra is the home of pure spirit. This chakra carries us beyond duality into the realm of oneness where we become united with our creator. Being in harmony with our creator and the universe is the ultimate goal of spirituality. It is the ultimate message of all mythology, and the ultimate desire behind most of our actions. As humans we long consciously or unconsciously to experience the bliss we once knew, the bliss of wholeness – total absorption in the divine. We are tiny drops of divinity, like rivers we flow towards our source. Rivers flow to the sea; we flow to the divine.

We constantly search for wholeness. Each step we take on life's long journey brings us closer to our creator. We may appear to step away from our divine path yet all steps eventually lead us forward. Even the most horrific and tragic happenings can lead to peace. It is in the darkness that light shines brightest. When things get really low and we become totally disillusioned with life and the material gains it offers we search for something more. We want to know the reason for our pain. Now we are ready to speak with the director of our life. We are forced to stop looking outside of ourselves and find the spirit within. When we look within we find the bliss of the divine.

Illness, death of a loved one, fear, pain and loss can all introduce us to an inner peace that we never knew before, because they deliver the message of what life is really about. Life is a one-way journey towards our divine creator. All the ups and downs are just stops along the way where we learn more of life's lessons to move us forward.

It is at the crown chakra that we eventually find peace. Here, where everything is still, we become the pure spirit we have been looking for. At the crown chakra we become whole again. We are totally embraced by our Creator. This union creates the lasting bliss we long for. In oneness we can simply Be.

Crown – Mind

When we transcend duality into the realm of oneness at the crown chakra, mind no longer exists in the same way. We are now in the realm of universal consciousness, the all-knowing mind. In the sacred Sanskrit language, this is known as Satchitananda – knowledge truth and bliss. This is the experience of knowing the truth and residing in its bliss. *I am* is the statement of the crown chakra.

Everything except absolute bliss takes us out of the crown chakra and returns us to duality. We can only *know* the experience of the crown chakra. We cannot really think about it, understand it or talk about it. When we do we return to duality. To talk about an experience separates us from it. The crown is simply about Being. It must be experienced for you to know it.

I believe we have all known the bliss of the crown chakra at some point in our lives. It is this knowledge that keeps us searching. We all know what it is simply to Be. *Can you remember a time in your life when you felt at one? A time when you felt truly peaceful?* A moment where *no separation existed between you and nature, between you and your Creator, you felt lifted and held. At that point you knew you were part of the universe, one with everything around you. This can happen during meditation, when the chakras open and energy flows freely through your system. It can happen while walking by the sea or on a mountaintop, where the aura has space to fully expand. This can happen at any place where the individual mind can be still and your energy field can expand enough to touch universal consciousness – to touch heaven.* The psychologist, Abraham Maslow, wrote of something he called a peak experience, which takes place when all our needs are met and we can turn to the divine. I think the peak experience is that of the crown chakra opening and letting us *know heaven.*

Crown – Body

The crown chakra differs from the other chakras. In some traditions it is not called a chakra at all because it has a very subtle frequency. This centre transcends the physical body and controls the energy body. The energy body is made up of pathways and centres where energy flows.

152   Pure spirit flows through the energy body and animates the physical body, giving it life. Without pure spirit nothing would exist including you and I. Pure spirit gives rise to the life force, the breath of life that pours through us. The life force needs to move freely through the nadis and meridians in the energy body. Free movement of energy brings good health to the body and harmony to the entire system.

Crown – Ailments

Alienation Life in the fast lane of the material world can cause us to feel alienated from nature and our creator, particularly those of us who live in cities. After all, we are part of nature and need to tune to its rhythm to feel whole. When we no longer honour the power of the sun, or use the moon to light our way, or watch the seasons as they turn, we alienate ourselves from something great. When we no longer ask the Creator to guide us but feel we know our own way, eventually we become lost. We lack clarity and live in constant pain and confusion. We know an emptiness so deep we fear nothing can fill it. We long for rest and inner peace. When we feel this way, it is a message from the Creator calling us to return home. Calling us to rest in the bliss of our divine nature. Journeying through the chakras and working on each one individually can provide us with the bliss we search for.

Lack of spiritual direction The time we live in and our modern societies alienate spirit. Therefore it is no surprise that so many people suffer with spiritual crisis. Spiritual crisis is when you know there must be more to life but somehow can't find it. Nothing makes sense any more. The question you are constantly asking is why? Why can't I find happiness? Why don't I feel fulfilled from my oh so very good job? Why am I not satisfied now that I have everything? Spiritual crisis is when you feel let down by religion and let down by life itself. It is when you don't know the purpose of it all anymore. You have lost your direction in life. Your soul is not in it. In fact where is your soul, and what is its true purpose? Spiritual crisis causes you to stop for a moment and ask the ultimate questions, why am I here? And where am I going? This is the first stage of your transformation; the first stage of journeying towards the crown chakra and union with your Creator.

John Lennon's words beautifully sum up that moment of release when we step off the treadmill and start to simply Be.

> *I'm just sitting here watching the wheels go*
> *round and round.*
> *I really love to watch them roll,*
> *no longer riding on the merry go round*
> *I just had to let it goooooo!*

It is when we are willing to stop for a moment, that we can begin to connect with our true nature and start to follow our soul purpose.

Disorders of the nervous system – paralysis, multiple sclerosis, Alzheimer's disease, etc. Ailments of the nervous system are governed by the crown chakra. The pituitary gland, which is the body's master gland, works closely with the nervous system and also resonates with the crown chakra. Meditation on the crown centre can bring healing and help to rebalance the body's complex chemical make-up. Spiritual cleansing can be done using the colours white, gold or purple. These colours can provide peace and protection, even when physical illness remains. Healing refers to wholeness and not the absence of disease. People can be ill, yet healed, while people who have no physical ailment require healing.

Ways of Rebalancing the Crown Chakra

Journal work – Energetic Review and Descent

For this exercise you will need your journal or a few sheets of A4 paper.

Your journey from the root chakra to the crown is now complete. You have opened to spirit and connected with the energy that animates your entire being. I am sure that if you have practised the rebalancing exercises much has changed in your life and will continue to do so. Your connection to the divine is everlasting. Love and wisdom are your trusted friends.

At this point you are invited to descend the chakras, moving from the crown to the root. As you journey, record in word or image your experience of each centre.

Begin by sitting upright with eyes closed and allow yourself to enter a meditative state. Breathe easily and relax your entire being.

1   *Take your attention to your crown chakra. Focus on its colour, its vibration and any sensations that you feel. Enter deep into the experience. Maintain your focus for at least five minutes.*

2   *What message is here for you today? See it unfold before you. What have you learnt so far? What do you now know?*

155

3   *Take your journal and draw/paint your*
     crown chakra. Write any key words.
     Try not to let your attention dissipate,
     but remain focused.

Repeat steps 1 to 3 at each chakra.

As you return to the root chakra, regain a sense of grounding. Feel the earth under your body as you open your whole being to the energy that floods through you. Let your body be alive and your mind quiet, feel the pulse of spirit as it speaks. Let the secrets of life be revealed to you. Accept your great blessing and give thanks.

Crown Chakra Meditation

Your ascension is complete, you have arrived at the crown chakra, the thousand-petalled lotus that blossoms beyond duality. This is the home of pure spirit. Meditation on pure spirit brings unity and liberation.

Arrange and cleanse your sacred space. Lift the energy with incense and essential oils. Burn gold, violet or white candles. Sit before a candle and stare into its shining flame. Know that nothing separates you from the light of the candle, all is made from pure vibrating energy. You are pure vibrational energy.

• *With your eyes closed, your back upright and body*
  comfortable, enter the sacred space inside your Self –
  the place where nothing changes, everything is still
  and silent. This place is deep, deep, inside you, it is
  the very core of your being. It is the still central hub
  of the spinning chakras. This central core runs from

the base chakra to the crown. It connects earth to heaven. It connects you with your Creator.

- *As you enter this space everything as you know it comes to an end. Earth, water, fire, air, ether, light, all cease to exist. There is no movement of energy, only pure undifferentiated energy, having no shape or form. There is nothing to fear, we originate from this very place, we know it well. But choose to forget.*

- *Let your spirit be re-united with the universal energy. Let your self plunge into nothingness, reach beyond the stars, complete the circle and dwell at peace in its centre.*

- *You are a part of the infinite vastness of the Divine Ocean. Be still and know that you are Divine.*

You are Everything

Your ascent through the chakras is now complete but your journey continues.

Give thanks. Blessed be.

TWELVE

BALANCE &

Integration

For ease of study we have explored the chakras individually. But having read this far, especially if you have been working with your chakras, you will know that they do not exist independently. Instead, they operate as a dynamic whole, each one affecting the others. It is important that the chakra system is viewed as a complex, integrated whole. Energy constantly flows from the crown chakra to the root and back again. It is for us to allow this energy to flow uninterrupted. Each chakra is open all the time. So we have the potential to tune to the vibration of every chakra and let them resonate fully with the universe.

Each chakra within an individual works in concert with the other chakras in that person. Each person's chakras interact with other people's chakras. And the chakras of people interact to create society's unique chakra system, which then relates to the chakra system of other cultures and societies. Wow! Read that again slowly and contemplate the complexity. Our chakras are resonating with other chakras all the time. The more harmonious the resonance is, the better we feel. We like the vibrations (vibes) of some people and places and we feel uncomfortable with others. Some people lift our vibrations while others make us feel drained and low. This is not our imagination, it is a very real energetic effect.

The chakras of different cultures meet and form the earth's chakra system, which we live in. This energy vibrates within the *evolutionary chakra system* of our time. And what is important right now, in evolutionary terms, is that we are entering the heart chakra, which is a time of major transformation. We are moving beyond the power conflicts of the solar plexus into the realm of love and compassion characterized by the heart chakra. This time is also known as the Aquarian age. We all have an important role to play if the planet is successfully to achieve this major transformation from the solar plexus to the heart chakra.

Our aim as individuals is to encourage the even flow of energy throughout each of our chakras. Even distribution of energy leads to harmony and it all starts within. We can change the world and create world peace; finding inner peace is the ideal starting place. It is only when we all recognize our essence as *absolute bliss* that peace will reign as the dominant experience of human kind. Each one of us makes a difference. When I know peace, I can share it with you; you will feel it emanate from my energy system. When you know peace you will carry it with you and others will feel it. As more people in our society balance their chakras, society will change; as society changes it will create a new resonance with the other societies and nations it meets. Eventually the peace we all desire will prevail in our world. Although many of us experience isolation, energy-wise there is no isolation. We are all connected through our energy fields. An energy shift in one person affects us all. Therefore, if we can create harmonious energy within ourselves we can create harmony everywhere.

Openness in one chakra facilitates the flow of energy through the centres above and below. If energy is restricted in the solar plexus chakra, you can expect to find limited energy in the sacral centre and the heart. So as you work with your chakra system pay close attention to how each centre relates to the others. For example, do you have lots of ideas and never seem to put them into action? This would suggest lots of energy in your solar plexus and third eye that cannot be grounded at the root chakra. Maybe energy is not flowing well through your sacral centre? Your sense of self may be distorted, causing low self-esteem and lack of commitment.

161

Do you lack time and space in your life and never seem to have enough energy for spiritual practice? You may need more energy flowing through your throat chakra and less in your root chakra.

Do you lack direction, yet manage to get things done when you have clarity? Maybe you need more energy in the universal chakras and less in your personal centres.

There are many relationships between the chakras, which unfortunately are beyond the introductory level of this book. See the further reading section for guidance on books. You may find it helpful to contact a professional healer or spiritual guide, who can personally assist you as you begin to understand where your energy is overflowing and where it is deficient. The chakra system is very complex and it takes a lot of practice to really get to know the fluctuations in your energy field. Change is the very nature of energy and your energy will differ on a daily basis. The more you practise the rebalancing exercises and keep a journal, as a record of your progress, the quicker and easier it will be to read what is taking place in your energy field at any given time. This way you can respond appropriately to life situations rather than react inappropriately. I scan my chakras and get an accurate reading in a few minutes, but that has taken years of practice. It is like sailing a ship on stormy seas; at first we have no idea how to find calm. We are sure that, without the grace of God, we will sink. With experience we learn to read the clouds and the elements, we know how long a storm will last and which way it will blow, we can safely assess the situation and instead of waiting we can sail through the storm directing ourselves towards calm waters. Through the chakras we can enter the very core of our being and programme our energy for physical, emotional and spiritual health. With experience we can assess energy as it ebbs and flows, learning to sail through stormy seas towards calm waters. We often forget that we can work with the Creator.

Health is dependent on the free flow of energy through all your chakras. The ultimate goal of chakra work is balance, seeking to connect with both the earth below and the sky above. Embodiment – enjoying life in a physical body – is as important as enlightenment – experiencing our spiritual nature. Seek always to embody the life of the spirit and free the life of the body.

As you continue working on the chakras let spirit, love and creativity guide you. I trust you will feel inspired and uplifted.

We are all part of the Divine plan. I hope that as you have journeyed through your chakras your Divine purpose has been revealed to you. I trust that you will continue to walk in love and light knowing that ....

You are truly blessed.

FURTHER
Reading

WAY of

There are a growing number of books on the chakras. These are six books that I personally recommend for enhancing your knowledge on the chakra system.

Caroline Shola Arewa Opening to Spirit
(Thorsons, 1998)

This book is a multi-cultural, in-depth exploration of the chakra system. I detail the aura, the elements and mythology as they relate to the chakras. *Opening to Spirit* is also a chakra workbook offering meditations, rituals and ways of working with essential oils, colour and crystals. This book has all you need to continue working on your chakras.

Harish Johari Chakras *(Destiny Books, 1987)*

Johari draws on the Sanskrit roots of the chakras. This is an excellent book for teachers and students of yoga.

Anodea Judith Wheels of Life
(Llewellyn, 1987 – new edition 1999)

An in-depth book on many aspects of the chakras.

Rosalyn Bruyere Wheels of Light
(Simon and Schuster, 1989)

An overview of the chakra system with a main focus on the root chakra.

Denese Shervington & Billie Jean Pace
Soul Quest *(Crown Trade Paperbacks, NY,
1994)*

This book is both powerful and beautiful. It offers a journey of healing for women of the African Diaspora.

Barbara A Brennan Hands of Light
(Bantam Books, 1987)

The author is a healer and a scientist. This is a classic book on healing with useful information on the chakras.

SPIRIT
Matters

WAY of

Caroline Shola Arewa is the founder/director of **Inner Vision**, a centre for personal and spiritual development. The centre offers training, workshops and seminars in stress management, healing, yoga and chakra psychology for individuals, groups and organizations. You can also visit Shola's website *SpiritMatters for Healthy Living.*

Caroline Shola Arewa can be contacted at:

>   *Inner Vision*
>   *PO Box 22032*
>   *London SW2 2WJ*
>
>   *E-mail: shola@shola.co.uk*
>   *www.shola.co.uk*
>   *www.spirit-matters.net*

By the same author:

Opening To Spirit

Contacting the healing power of the chakras and honouring African spirituality

Opening to Spirit is an in-depth exploration of the ancient chakra system. Caroline Shola Arewa draws on a wealth of spiritual wisdom and mythology from Ancient Egypt, Early India and West Africa to create a healing process that will help you raise your awareness, develop greater soul consciousness and claim your spiritual inheritance.

This book:

- *reveals the mysteries of the aura and the ancient chakra system and makes them accessible for every day use*
- *introduces you to the African deities, including those of creation, truth and sensuality*
- *describes techniques for cleansing and balancing the chakras*
- *explores the healing power of meditation and ritual*
- *offers tools for self-discovery, physical health and spiritual fulfilment*
- *explores the five elements – ether, air, fire, water and earth*
- *explains the planetary rhythms and the ancient cosmological laws of nature in relation to the chakras.*

ISBN: 0 7225 3726 3

Way of Reincarnation

Judy Hall

Over half the world's population accept reincarnation – they believe they have lived before and will do so again. In the East this is taken for granted, while in the West the belief is rapidly gaining acceptance once again. This comprehensive introduction looks at world thought and contains all the information you need to gain an in-depth knowledge of reincarnation, including:

- *what reincarnation is*
- *its cultural and religious background*
- *how the soul reincarnates*
- *famous people throughout history and their beliefs in reincarnation*
- *the evidence for and against reincarnation.*

Judy Hall is an internationally known author, lecturer and workshop leader and has been a karmic counsellor for 25 years. She has written numerous books on reincarnation and has frequently appeared on radio and television in the UK and US to discuss the subject.

ISBN: 0 00 710290 9

Way of Natural Magic

Nigel Pennick

Natural magic is a way of working with the vital energy around us, including that which comes from our own awareness and intention. Working with natural magic involves simple but powerful practical techniques that anyone can use to bring more magic into their everyday lives. This comprehensive introduction contains all the information you need to gain an in-depth knowledge of magic including:

- *an explanation of earth, mineral, and plant magic*
- *magic animals and how we can work with them*
- *the power within – the magic of the human body*
- *the magic of the land, of food and drink*
- *natural magic charms, talismans and amulets – what they are and how to make and empower them.*

Nigel Pennick has conducted research on ancient monuments, folk traditions, geomancy and magic for over 25 years. In 1975 he founded the Institute of Geomantic Research. He has worked all over Europe, Canada and the US and is a leading author in this field.

ISBN: 0 7225 4038 8

Way of Tibetan Buddhism

Lama Jampa Thaye

Buddhism is now one of the fastest growing spiritual practices in the West. Tibetan Buddhism is a branch of Buddhism that places particular emphasis on the teacher-disciple relationship which lies at the heart of the spiritual life. This comprehensive introduction contains all the information you need to gain an in-depth knowledge of Tibetan Buddhism, including:

- *what Tibetan Buddhism is and how it developed*
- *an insight into all the basic teachings including Indian, Tibetan and Western practice*
- *the historical background to Buddhism*
- *a summary of the major schools.*

Lama Jampa Thaye (David Stott) is a lecturer in the Religions and Theology Department of Manchester University and a Vajrayona teacher in the Sakya and Kagyu Buddhist traditions, having studied under various masters for over three decades. He is the principal disciple of Karma Thinley Rinpoche, the Director of the Dechen Community in Europe, and the author of a number of books on Buddhism.

ISBN: 0 7225 4017 5

Way of Crystal Healing

Ronald Bonewitz

From one of the world's leading crystal experts, this is the best introduction available for an easy to read and sensible beginners guide to crystals. As well as giving a thorough introduction to the properties and qualities of crystals, this book explores how crystal healing works, and how it can be combined with related therapies such as acupuncture, chakra work and energy healing.

The book stands out for its very grounded, realistic approach. The author believes that many properties are attributed to crystals that they simply can't have, and that much of the information available to the public comes from misinformed sources. This book will give the beginner an honest understanding of the real value of crystals and of how they can develop their personal experiences of working with them.

Ronald Bonewitz originally trained as a geologist specializing in crystal chemistry, and now holds a PhD in Behavioural Science, emphasizing physiological pyschology. With a reputation for clarity and integrity, he has given hundreds of crystal courses worldwide and has written several books on crystals.

ISBN: 0 00 710392 1

Be initiated into a new Way of life

Also available in the Thorsons Way of series:

Way of Wicca (new edition)	Vivianne Crowley	0-00-711022-7
Way of Zen (new edition)	Martine Batchelor	0-00-712001-X
Way of Tarot (new edition)	Evelyne Herbin and Terry Donaldson	0-00-711018-9
Way of Reiki (new edition)	Kajsa Krishni Borang	0-00-711019-7
Way of Meditation (new edition)	Christina Feldman	0-00-711684-5
Way of NLP (new edition)	Joseph O'Connor and Ian McDermott	0-00-711020-0
Way of Psychic Protection (new edition)	Judy Hall	0-00-711021-9